For Bess

A Primer on
PRODUCTIVITY

A Primer on

The Primer series is under the editorial supervision of
PETER L. BERNSTEIN

PRODUCTIVITY

Solomon Fabricant

 RANDOM HOUSE   New York

Introduction

There is no telling what the big economic issue of the day will be when this *Primer on Productivity* appears in print. But whatever the focal point of current public interest in economic matters, it is a sure bet that productivity will be involved either directly or indirectly.

Why so sure? Because facts on productivity are among the fundamental facts of economic life. Productivity touches us all as citizens, employees, employers, or consumers.

Let me illustrate:

Item:—When the President (or if not he, then one of his critics) asks that wages and prices toe the line, it is to some sort of "productivity guideline" that he is pointing. "Productivity, which used to lead a quiet life in economic textbooks, is a fighting word in Washington these days," is how *Business Week* once phrased it.

Item:—When automation is welcomed by some and feared by others, what these people have on their minds is the effects of increased productivity. Automation can ease a worker's burden and help raise his wages—which is welcome. Automation can also throw people out of their jobs and make their skills obsolete—which is not at all welcome.

Item:—When Soviet leaders stare into the future and imagine Russia's output surpassing that of the United States, they are also thinking of productivity. In fact, they hang their hopes on Russia's productivity growing faster than ours. To this end they plan the lives of the Russian masses and exhort them with Lenin's words that "the productivity of labor is, in the final analysis, the most important, the main tool for the victory of the new order." The Russians have often fooled themselves—and others—about the best way to increase productivity and about their success in doing so, but on the importance of productivity their thinking has been kept straight. "In the final analysis" it is indeed higher labor productivity that makes for more production and thus also for more national power.

In fact, anywhere and everywhere when men struggle to make a better life for themselves and their children, it is higher productivity more than harder labor on which they must rely. In this war, too—a war far greater and much, much older than our generation's hot and cold wars—the importance of productivity is recognized. The high productivity level of the United States is the envy not only of the Russians and their satellites but also of the "unaligned" countries of Asia and Africa. They also want to raise their low standards of living, and they seek the help of both sides in speeding up this development.

Western countries already "developed" also know that the best way to raise income levels further is to concentrate on productivity. Right after World War II they began sending scores of "working parties" over to the United States to learn how so high a productivity level was attained in this country. And Europe still worries about the "technological gap" between them and us.

Put more generally, productivity measurements are addressed to important questions. In one sense, productivity measures the fruitfulness of human labor under varying circumstances. In another sense, it measures the efficiency with which resources as a whole—capital as well as manpower—are employed in production. In still another sense, it measures the forces that underlie the trends of real wages and of relative prices. And, finally, it measures a major factor in the determination of labor requirements and thus of employment.

A better understanding of productivity can help us resolve the many issues that are raised by these questions. Too often, fruitful discussion is hampered by confusion over just what productivity is, how fast it is growing, what its sources and its consequences are, and how best to encourage its advance. Although research in this field has by no means turned up all the answers, enough is known about productivity to make the knowledge of significant value to all affected by it.

To provide this knowledge is the objective of this book. It is labeled a primer. This simply means that technical terms have been avoided and that the text has been kept as free as possible of the arrays of statistics, the pages of charts, and the rows of mathematical equations that economists need to use. For the present purpose, none of these is necessary. The essential findings can be given in language that is plain, yet not written down to the level of superficiality. This is a primer, yes; but it is a primer for people who want a serious treatment of a subject intimately related to the economic welfare of all of us.

Contents

PART I

Basic Facts on Productivity

CHAPTER I

What Productivity Is

Why should there be any question about the meaning and measurement of productivity? Why, when labor and management meet to discuss wages, do they get into arguments over productivity (among other things)? Or when productivity levels or growth in this country are compared with productivity levels or growth abroad —in Russia, say, or the Common Market countries— why are different answers possible? Or when productivity guideposts for prices are considered, why do opinions clash on which measurement of productivity is appropriate and sometimes, as well, on whether *any* productivity guidepost is appropriate?

Productivity refers to a comparison between the quantity of goods or services produced and the quantity of resources employed in turning out these goods or services. When the same resources that were employed in the past now produce more than they did before, we agree that productivity has increased. Obviously, attempts to establish whether and how much productivity is changing take into account the relationship between what comes *out* of production and what goes *into* production, that is, the ratio between *output* and *input*. But we can compare output with man-hour input, or with the total of labor and capital input, or with something in between. The results are different, and the meaning of these several kinds of output-input comparisons is different. Although all productivity measurements are addressed to important questions, some of the questions are best answered with one kind of productivity measurement and others with another kind. Not always being clear on this, people occasionally use the wrong productivity measurement for the particular purpose they have in mind.

A second reason for differences of opinion in dealing with productivity is that people are human and self-interest may influence their choice of productivity measurement. Thus, even though a group may know the appropriate measurement in a given situation, they may try to use one that best strengthens their own case— for example, for or against a wage or price increase. Those on the other side may resist, or they may have already tried the same trick with productivity measurements best suited to *their* ends. Controversy is then inevitable.

Third, even when the purpose and meaning are quite sharp and clear and everything is aboveboard, productivity comparisons made between periods far apart, or between countries dissimilar in resources, consumption habits, and economic organization, will yield more than one answer. These may sometimes be very different. Television sets, for example, were not produced in 1900 and are still not produced or even used in some countries today. Broiler chickens are of better quality now than a few decades ago and better in this country than elsewhere. A pint of wine may be equal (in market value) to two pints of beer in one country or period and to more or less than two pints in another country or period. These differences raise difficulties in the measurement of a nation's or an industry's output. Similar difficulties arise in measuring total input—that is, in combining man-hours of different quality and "machine-hours" of pieces of capital equipment of different character, size, and vintage to get a measure of the services of labor and capital.

The way in which we meet these and other such difficulties will, to some degree, determine the results when, for example, we compare productivity in the United States today with that of 1900, or when we compare our present productivity with that of Russia or India. There is no clear consensus or opinion among economists and statisticians on just which is the right way. They may try different ways to see how close the results are and then follow the convention of averaging the different figures. But it is a convention that people might reject when they do not like the results. And there is always more than one way to average figures. Fortunately, in most comparisons different methods give close answers. This is not always so, however, and I expect the reader will be surprised by some of the differences that will be shown in later chapters.

A fourth reason for differences in the measurement of productivity is that statistics on output and input are limited in quantity and quality. How the gaps are filled or which of several conflicting pieces of evidence is chosen will affect the results. It is therefore not surprising that the steelworkers' union can come up with one index of productivity for the steel industry, the management with another, and when government gets involved, there may be a third. These different indexes need not be very far apart for controversy to arise. A difference of just a few tenths of a point may prove to be a stumbling block to agreement when it means even a few cents, more or less, in a wage package.

Finally, when one talks about the growth or trend of productivity, it makes a difference whether one measures the trend over a five-year period or a ten-year period, and which five- or ten-year period. For example, many people were startled in 1966 when the Council of Economic Advisers shifted its basis for calculating productivity guidelines from the average rate of growth over the preceding five years to the average rate of growth over a rather different period. It made a significant difference—otherwise, why the shift?—and we shall see how much in Chapter II.

We will meet the differences among various productivity measurements as we turn in succession to each of the aspects of our subject. Of those mentioned, the most important is the first, the difference that arises because productivity measurements are put to different uses. It is also the most complicated. On both counts, therefore, it merits further explanation at this point.

Productivity is defined in various ways because we have various questions in mind when we ask how productivity is doing. Unless we are more specific, the figures offered in response to our question will vary.

There are, in fact, two main concepts and measurements of productivity that may be—and are—used. We must be careful to distinguish between them and understand what each actually spells out for us, for without this understanding we could be like the blind men who went away with different impressions of what an elephant is. Also, with these two main concepts clearly in mind, we will be better able to understand certain other variations that will crop up in our discussions of wages and prices.

In the first of these concepts, output is compared with the simple sum of all the hours of labor—the "man-hours"—spent in production. We thus take into account not only the number of persons engaged but also the hours put in by each of them and make allowance for differences between countries or periods in the length of the workweek or work-year. This concept, which is usually expressed as "output per man-hour" or as "labor productivity," is the one we use when we ask: How many more units of output—more now than before, or more here than there—are we getting from an hour of work done? The answer tells us the fruitfulness of human labor under varying circumstances—circumstances that may be as different, in terms of labor quality, amount of equipment, scale of output, methods of production, and so on, as the 1960's are from the 1860's or as the United States is from India. Output per man-hour or labor productivity seems simple enough, but its meaning is not at all simple, as we shall see.

In the second main concept of productivity, output is compared with total input—that is, with all the resources employed in production, each appropriately weighted. The term we shall use is "output per unit of labor and capital" or, more briefly, "total productivity." (Frequently used, but perhaps less clear, is the term "total factor productivity.") Total resources include not only manpower, measured simply by number of man-hours, but also the intangible capital invested in educa-

tion to improve the quality of labor and the tangible
capital invested in plant, equipment, tools and rolling
stock, land and mines, and inventories of all sorts—and
still other forms of intangible and tangible capital—
without which an hour of labor would yield far less than
it does. Indeed, many of the goods and services we depend on today could not be produced at all without the
assistance of this capital.

Total input is measured by the sum of "weighted
man-hours" and "weighted machine-hours." Weighted
man-hours differ from the unweighted man-hours used
in calculating output per man-hour because an hour of
high-quality labor—a highly paid man-hour of work—
counts for proportionately more in the weighted aggregate than a low-quality hour of labor—a lower wage
man-hour. In this way, we take account of the differences
in skill, education, length of experience, and other factors determining the quality of labor. Thus also, account
is taken of the intangible capital invested to improve
the quality of labor. We calculate weighted machine-
hours similarly. (The reader should understand that
machine-hours is shorthand for the hours worked by all
kinds of tangible capital.) The sum of weighted man-
hours and weighted machine-hours, then, is an aggregate in which hours of labor and hours of tangible
capital are counted more heavily when they are worth
more in terms of wages or salaries or rental values; conversely, they are counted less heavily when their hourly
earnings or hourly rental values are low.

This second concept of output per unit of labor and
capital, or total productivity, is the one we use when
we ask: How many more units of output are we getting
from a unit of labor and capital combined? The answer

tells us how efficiently resources as a whole, capital as well as labor, are employed in production.

Each of the two concepts contributes to a better understanding of the economic world. But they are not interchangeable. They tell us different things about it, and they have different uses. Both cannot make sense as a guidepost for wages, for example. The concepts must therefore be sharply distinguished, and it is for this reason that they are tagged with different labels.

When we compare output with the simple sum of man-hours—unweighted man-hours—it is correct to call the relationship labor productivity as we do here for brevity's sake. But we must not read such a comparison to mean that wage earners, or all workers combined, are wholly responsible for productivity levels and for increases, for this is not the case.

Similarly, when we compare output with a combination of weighted man-hours and machine-hours, it is correct to call the relationship total productivity and to say that it measures efficiency in the use of labor and capital, as we do. But we must exercise care in this case too, for a different reason. The sum of weighted man-hours and tangible capital hours is only an approximation of the correct total input. The services of certain types of intangible capital are omitted from the total because we cannot count them.

It is interesting that as we move from the first to the second concept, we pass to a higher degree of sophistication in our measurements. Output per man-hour requires less information and is easier to calculate. Output per unit of labor and capital, because it requires more information, is the more complex measurement. It is also of more recent vintage and is less frequently available than the relatively simple output per man-hour.

However, the productivity measurement that is more complex in terms of information required is less complex in terms of content or meaning. More, not less, is told by output per man-hour than by output per unit of labor and capital. To demonstrate this, let us look at the two concepts again, but this time in reverse order.

A change in output per unit of labor and capital tells us whether efficiency in the conversion of labor and capital into output is rising or falling. A rise or fall in efficiency may result from changes in technology, in size and character of economic organization, in management skills, and in a host of other determinants. These changes in efficiency in the use of resources cannot be determined by comparing a change in output with a change in labor alone or capital alone. For example, output per unit of just plant and equipment may be falling, yet efficiency will be rising if there is a saving of labor's services per unit of product, and if this saving of labor exceeds the increase in the services of capital used per unit of product. Similarly, a rise in output per man-hour will overstate the increase in efficiency if some of the savings in man-hours result from an investment in capital—that is, from a substitution of labor by capital.

A change in output per man-hour, then, reflects the combined effect of a change in two things. One is a change in efficiency in the sense just mentioned, as it is measured by output per unit of total input. The other is a change in the volume of tangible and intangible capital per man-hour or, more exactly, a change in the volume of services of capital relative to the volume of services of plain labor.

Because we shall consider tangible capital separately from intangible "human capital" when we inquire into the sources of increases in labor productivity, it is better to formulate these statements a little differently. Let us say, then, that a change in output per man-hour reflects the combined effect of a change in *three* things: first, in the efficiency with which labor and capital are used; second, in the amount of tangible capital employed with each man-hour of labor; and third, in the average quality of labor. Output per man-hour will rise if efficiency rises, even if tangible and intangible capital per man-hour remains unchanged. Output per man-hour will also rise if tangible or intangible capital per man-hour rises, even if efficiency remains unchanged. Consequently, output per man-hour will reflect the net result of the three possible changes (each given its proper weight).

In the normal course of economic development, output per man-hour rises because all three—efficiency, labor quality, and tangible capital per man-hour—go up. But let us not jump ahead of our story. With the main concepts and terminology defined, we are ready to turn to the basic facts on productivity. We begin with the trend of national productivity in the United States.

CHAPTER II

The Trend of National Productivity

The trend of productivity, we have learned, is really a pair of trends defined in two different ways. Each is worth looking at, for each presents a meaningful aspect of our country's economic growth.

What do we see in the record of the years since 1889, the period for which our information is most adequate?

First, national output in relation to total resources, our index of output per unit of labor and capital, grew at an average annual rate of 1.7 percent. This tells us that productivity in the sense of efficiency in the use of the country's resources—including among those resources unskilled workers, skilled workers, and professionals (and also including the intangible capital invested in their education and training) and the tangible capital invested in plant and equipment—has improved greatly.

Second, national output in relation to man-hours of labor alone, lumped together without regard to grade or quality—our index of output per man-hour or labor productivity—grew at an average rate of 2.4 percent per annum. This tells us that the output yielded by an hour's work has risen half again as fast as efficiency. Had tangible and intangible capital per man-hour remained unchanged, labor productivity could not have risen faster than efficiency. The fact that it did means that capital per man-hour went up. Labor productivity rose, in other words, not only because of increased efficiency, but also because of more investment in tangible capital and in education, training, and other improvements in the quality of our labor supply. Thus we must understand that the rise in labor productivity, the most widely used measure of productivity, reflects *all* these developments, not just one of them. It is the combination of them that resulted in the annual rise of 2.4 percent in national output per man-hour.

Of course, these figures are estimates, with all the limitations of estimates. But despite the qualifications, there is no doubt about the substantial rates at which both total productivity and labor productivity have grown in the United States over the past eighty years.

Indeed, we may rightly call the average annual increase of 1.7 percent in total productivity and 2.4 percent in labor productivity sharp—even remarkable—although to some readers even the higher figure, 2.4 percent per annum, may seem small. It is not. Such an average annual rate means an increase of 25 percent in a decade, a doubling in thirty years, and more than a sextupling over the eighty years covered by the estimate. The average worker in the United States today produces more than six times as much in an hour of work as did his grandfather or great-grandfather in 1889.

Very few countries have long-term records that look

as good as this. Further, because our *level* of labor productivity has always been very high by world standards, a 2.4 percent increase means a large *absolute* increase each year, judged by these same standards. Many countries would be very happy to have their current level of output per man-hour equal to the goods and services we now *add* to our output per man-hour in just a few years.

The long-term rates we have been looking at are averages that balance out any year-to-year fluctuations there may be in the rate of productivity increase. But productivity did in fact grow at an uneven rate. These shifts in the rate of growth are made up of a number of components, or different kinds of movements, that are worth distinguishing.

Among these movements, the cyclical fluctuations in productivity are most prominent. All through the period covered—before World War I, during the interwar years, and since World War II—the rate of productivity growth has fluctuated with the general state of business. (We shall see why in a later chapter.) The imprint of business cycles on labor productivity would be especially pronounced were output to be compared with the man-hours that might be supposed to be "available" for work under conditions of full employment. But the effect of business cycles is visible even in the more usual comparisons of output with the man-hours actually worked—the index of output per man-hour. And the effect of business cycles can also be seen, as we would expect, when we compare output with the combination of man-hours actually worked and machine-hours available for work—our index of output per unit of labor and capital. (Information on machine-hours actually worked is not available.) Measured either way, year-to-year rises in productivity have been greater than the long-term rate of increase in productivity when business was generally expanding, and less (often falling) when business was generally contracting.

Year-to-year changes in productivity were appreciably influenced not only by business cycles but also by random factors, although some of these irregular changes merely reflect the inadequacies of the figures. Productivity change is measured by the ratio of two indexes, output and input, each subject to error; and even slight errors in each of these will sometimes combine to produce considerable error in the ratio, just as they will sometimes cancel out. Thus we cannot always be sure that a fluctuation in the rate of change between particular pairs of years is more than the result of statistical error. On the other hand, the fairly systematic business cycle behavior that we see suggests that the errors are not overwhelming. We know, also, that some of the irregularities are real. They reflect the impact of weather, strikes, and the other random factors to which life is subject.

Beyond the short-term fluctuations in productivity growth due to business cycles and random factors, longer-term changes show up when one looks at the year-to-year statistics. These include occasional spurts and slowdowns in productivity growth that extend over a period of years. The data for the period beginning in 1889, on which we have been relying, and rougher data available for earlier years back to the Civil War suggest something like five long waves in the trend rate of change in productivity. High average rates of increase in productivity, measured over a decade or more, alternated with low average rates of increase. But even the low rates, it should be stressed, were always rates of increase, not of decline. In output per man-hour, the upward trend rates ranged from a low of about 1 percent per annum during the ten- or fifteen-year period centered around 1910 or 1915 to a high of about 3.5 percent during the decade immediately following World War II.

Did the highest trend rate appear in a recent period and the lowest appear in a period now half a century distant because the rate of growth of labor productivity has been accelerating? That is, has labor productivity been growing at a rate that rises more or less systematically from period to period, so that we may reasonably —and with some confidence—project a higher rate in the period ahead than in the present period? The question is important both for understanding the past and for looking into the future, for national plans in general and wage and price contracts in particular are often set for several years ahead. And it is a question on which some people hold decided opinions.

We have already seen that labor productivity did not rise at anything like a steady rate in the past. If we refuse to blink our eyes at these fluctuations, we must answer the question in the negative. We may reasonably expect labor productivity to continue to rise—exceptions have been few in the past—but that we may expect it to rise faster in the next few years is much more doubtful.

But suppose we ignore the fluctuations and focus on the underlying trend. What can we say then? Reasons have often been given for expecting labor productivity to rise more rapidly in the future. The exploitation of technological "breakthroughs" in atomic energy, electronics, and automation, and the heavy investment by government and private interests in education and research and development, for example, make up a plausible case. But we can also list negative factors, ranging from water and other shortages to congestion in city streets. And expectations regarding the speed with which new technologies will be exploited can be overoptimistic, as was the case with atomic energy right after World War II. The positive might well overpower the negative factors, but we cannot be sure. Because we do not know their respective weights, we do not know how they add up on net balance.

What we can do is to look at the historical record, smooth out the fluctuations, and see how the underlying trend has behaved.

A few years ago, the U.S. Bureau of Labor Statistics attempted to discern the trend in just that way. The procedure involved comparing a growth curve that assumes acceleration in the rate of growth in output per manhour with the actual course taken by output per manhour over the period available. The assumed curve seemed to fit the facts reasonably well. Unfortunately, the period covered by the B.L.S. index ran only from 1909 to 1958. This meant, first, that the earliest period covered by the B.L.S.—the period centered about 1915 —was one in which labor productivity was rising at an unusually *low* trend rate. It meant, second, that the final period covered—the immediate post-World War II decade—was one in which labor productivity was rising at an unusually *high* rate. The assumption of acceleration, therefore, does fit the period 1909–58 fairly well. But it is inconsistent with the period before 1909, when labor productivity rose more rapidly than during the B.L.S.'s initial period, and after 1958, when labor productivity rose less rapidly than during the B.L.S.'s final period.

This is made clear when we extend the B.L.S. output per man-hour series for 1909–58 forward to 1966 and back to 1889 (using the only available series, that of the National Bureau of Economic Research) and then compare it with the extrapolated growth curve assumed by the B.L.S.—extrapolated forward and backward, of course, on a basis consistent with the B.L.S. assumptions. Expectations based on the assumption of acceleration—such as those voiced by Walter Reuther when he testified before the Joint Economic Committee of the Congress early in 1959—were disappointed in the 1960's. The *projected* average rate of growth for 1959–66 was about 4 percent per annum, almost a third higher than the average rate *actually* experienced during 1959–66. Further, the particular growth curve used by the B.L.S. assumed such rapid acceleration as to imply a *declining* trend in labor productivity in the early 1890's. This implication is hardly consistent with the historical facts as we know them. Labor productivity actually rose at an average rate of 2.5 percent between 1889 and 1895.

In short, it is difficult to have any confidence in the assumption of acceleration. We can nevertheless be sure that labor productivity increased more rapidly, on the average, during the past thirty-five or forty years than it did during the preceding period of equal length. This change appears to represent a break in the trend however, rather than a gradual progression or series of shifts that may be expected to continue. Output per man-hour rose at an average annual rate of 2.1 percent between 1889 and the 1920's, the first half of the period covered, and at a rate of 2.8 percent during the second half, the years since the 1920's. The difference is there, whether we split the period early or late in the 1920's or right in the middle of the 1920's. The available statistics make it clear that the rate of growth in productivity witnessed by the present generation has been substantially higher than the rate experienced earlier.

This is an important fact. But it does not by itself imply, as would the fact of acceleration, that past changes should lead our generation to expect a still higher rate of growth in productivity in future years. This expectation *could* turn out to be justified as events unfold. Or it could not. What we know at present does not justify our counting on it.

Before we leave the national productivity indexes, I must repeat a few words of caution. These indexes, like all estimates, are surrounded by margins of error. This becomes evident when revisions are made. But even revised figures are still "subject to revision." And it is evident also when two independent estimates of the same quantity differ significantly, as do the B.L.S. and National Bureau of Economic Research estimates of labor productivity for 1909–16.

But there is more to it than just this. The estimated increase in labor productivity of 2.4 percent per annum, which I cited above, is for the private domestic economy alone. An alternative estimate, which I did not mention to avoid confusing the reader, is 2.1 percent per annum. This estimate relates to the *entire* American economy, which is what we really want. However, this lower figure includes an estimate for government, an estimate that is rather rough and therefore uncertain because of the difficulty of putting a figure on the quantity of services produced by government to meet collective wants. (This is so even when the estimate of national output used in the calculation is the so-called "peacetime version" of national output, from which national defense is excluded.) The higher figure, though more reliable, is for the private economy only, which is a very large part, but surely not the whole, of the national economy. Because the estimate for government probably understates the trend in government productivity, it would not be unreasonable to put the figures for the nation as a whole somewhere in the middle of the range shown —2.1 to 2.4 percent a year—and closer to the higher than the lower end. But economists have greater confidence in the estimates for the private economy, exclusive of government, and we see these estimates most frequently. Indeed, the "official" estimate of national output per man-hour made by the U.S. Bureau of Labor Statistics is for the private economy only.

I must add that even the estimate of output per man-hour for the private economy may be too low. All the measures of output—and thus also of productivity—fail to take adequate account of improvement in the quality of output. (However, in the case of output per unit of labor and capital, the downward bias in output may be more or less offset by a similar bias—already mentioned —in the measurement of total input.) Although the two estimates cited for labor productivity cannot be assumed to "bracket" the true figures, they do serve at least to underscore the limitations of all the estimates, official and unofficial. For general historical and analytical purposes, however, there is reason to believe that the available indexes are close enough to the mark. But this is not to say that they are always good enough to be used for other purposes, such as "directing" the course of wages and prices.

Another caution is necessary. Because the rate of increase in productivity has been far from uniform, neither producers nor users of productivity figures should talk about "the trend" without specifying the period from which they derive it. Trend rates derived from one period will differ, sometimes considerably, from those derived from a longer, or shorter, or altogether different period.

The trend used by the President's Council of Economic Advisers as a guideline during 1962–68 illustrates the need for both cautions. In the 1964 report of the council, when it was first presented "officially," the trend rate of increase in output per man-hour in the economy at large—the productivity guideline—was stated to be 3.2 percent per annum. It was based on the annual average percentage change in output per man-hour during 1958–63, the latest five years for which figures were available at the time. As the council saw it then, a five-year period would give a good approximation of the trend, because it would average out the ups and downs of cyclical productivity swings. The trend rate was also 3.2 percent during 1959–64. But then revisions in the estimates of national output by the Department of Commerce turned the estimates of annual change in output per man-hour for both 1958–63 and 1959–64 from 3.2 percent to 3.4—not a negligible difference when compounded over a period of time. Furthermore, by the end of 1965 the average rate of change during the preceding five years had risen from the revised 3.4 to 3.6 percent, because of the unusually long business expansion that began in 1961. The council thereupon decided to discard the original basis for calculating the trend rate and to hold to the 3.2 percent on a different basis —namely, that 3.2 percent per annum more closely measured the "true" long-term *sustainable* trend of productivity that we could expect to prevail in the future. As we have seen, the figure of 3.2 percent does approximate the average over the full post-World War II period. But that figure exceeds the average of 2.8 percent over the period since the 1920's and exceeds still more the average of 2.4 over the period since 1889. And we have learned that, in the past, periods of high trend rates alternated with periods of low trend rates. Hence, we had better be cautious with regard to extrapolations of recent past trends into the future, even when these trends are adjusted for cyclical swings. Extrapolations of trends, the record suggests, will always be risky.

The prime fact that emerges from all of this is that, with the passage of time, a given quantity of labor produces larger and larger quantities (and better qualities) of goods and services. We see a persistent and powerful tendency toward an increase in the volume of tangible and intangible capital available to each person at work and an improvement in the efficiency with which labor and capital are used in production. Sometimes the outcome was a fast, sometimes a slow, rate of growth in labor productivity. Occasionally, the tendency was entirely offset for a while by cyclical and random factors. But only once, namely, during the great business contraction of 1929–1933, was the interruption long enough to prevent labor productivity from reaching a new high within four years.

The persistence with which the nation's labor productivity has grown begins to tell us something of the reasons *why* it has grown. The facts on productivity in individual industries can also help us to understand this process. To these, therefore, we now turn our attention.

CHAPTER III

Productivity Differences among Industries

Rising trends in labor productivity constitute a *general* industrial phenomenon. This is the first fact that stands out from an analysis of individual industries. Every industry or industry group for which a reasonably adequate index is available for a period long enough to define a trend has experienced long-term growth in output per man-hour. This means that the upward trend in national labor productivity reflects more than an advance in a few "progressive" sectors of the economy, with other sectors marking time. Instead, the national trend reflects some degree of progress in *all* the sectors for which there is information—whether it be farming or mining, manufacturing or transportation, communications or gas and electric utilities.

To this first fact we may add two other general developments worth noting. One is the trend in the efficiency with which labor and capital are used. In this, too, a rising trend has been widespread. Output per unit of labor and capital, like output per man-hour, rose throughout American industry. Also interesting is the fact that in nearly all individual industries, as in the economy taken as a whole, output per man-hour has risen more rapidly than output per unit of labor and capital combined. This means that capital per man-hour also has risen in most industries.

Taken together, these developments tell us something about the sources of the increase in labor productivity in individual industries. In virtually all industries, we learn, the rise in labor productivity reflects both a rise in the amount of capital at work with each person and a rise in the efficiency with which labor and capital are used in production.

Another fact, though perhaps obvious, requires emphasis. Although it is correct to say that rises in efficiency and in capital per worker, and therefore also in labor productivity, are general phenomena found in industries throughout the nation, we can also see a great degree of variation among industries in the rates of rise. Labor productivity went up by a greater amount in some industries and by a lesser amount in others. At one end of the range of increase in output per man-hour during the first half of the century is the electric utility industry, with an increase of almost 2,500 percent, equal to an average rate of increase of 16 percent per year. At the other end is anthracite coal mining, with an increase in labor productivity of under 50 percent over the same period, or less than 1 percent per year. Similar differences, though less extreme, characterize the rates of increase in efficiency and in capital per man-hour.

These differences among industries in rates of increase in productivity are striking. They raise important questions about differences among industries in rates of change in wages and salaries, in prices, and in employment. For example, are industries in which labor productivity has risen very rapidly also those in which wage rates have risen rapidly or employment fallen rapidly? And what about wage rates and employment in industries with slow increases in labor productivity?

We will answer these questions in later chapters. Here we must deal with a different set of questions: Do the available indexes correctly portray developments in the United States? How good are the indexes? Is the sample of industries for which indexes have been computed reasonably representative of industries with slow as well as fast rates of growth? In other words, is the "general" phenomenon of rising productivity less general than what we observe in the available information? In an age when productivity statistics—not only for the nation as a whole but also for individual industries—are used to guide policy, such questions are crucial.

There are, of course, thousands of individual industries in a country as big and as economically advanced as the United States. For many of these individual industries, however, productivity indexes simply do not exist. The required statistics on output and input (especially capital input) are often entirely lacking; or they are given only in combination with the statistics of other industries; or they are not sufficiently detailed for use in indexes that deserve to be considered reasonably accurate. Many as are the gaps today, they are even more numerous when we try to observe long-term trends in productivity and must depend on the poorer statistics of earlier days.

It is for these reasons that we have indexes for only some thirty-odd industries going back as far as the turn of the century, and most of those are really *groups* of industries rather than industries as most people think of them. Those included are important, for among them are some of the largest industries or groups of industries in the country, as I have already noted. Yet even the total of manufacturing, agriculture, mining, and public utilities, the industries with good statistics, make up less than half the entire economy today, measured either by value of output or number of persons employed. Also, they are largely limited to the commodity-producing sectors, as the list indicates. Similar data are not available for the service industries, construction, trade, finance, and government. Although for recent decades productivity indexes have been calculated for the latter groups of industries, these shorter series are naturally less able to indicate long-term trends; and in any case they are much less reliable than in industries, such as manufacturing, for which statistics have been collected for a long time and have had a chance to become "seasoned." The estimate for government, we have already seen, is so weak—it virtually assumes no increase in labor productivity—that the official index of national labor productivity relates only to the private economy, not to the entire nation.

Yet all the evidence on historical changes in industrial organization and technology over the past half century or more indicates that labor productivity has increased not only in the industries covered by the long-term statistics but also in the service and other industries not covered. Physicians, for example, were among the first to buy automobiles and install telephone service, with obvious effects on their productivity. In retail trade, a source of increased labor productivity has been prepackaging, which has spread even to the vegetable and meat departments of food stores, thus shifting a good deal of the work of the salesclerks to the slow hours of the retail day or out of the store altogether and into the factory. Even in government, electrical devices are now reading census schedules, preparing fiscal accounts, and catching up with scofflaws who prefer to ignore parking tickets. Such information cannot tell us how much labor or total productivity has grown in the service trades, government, or the other omitted industries, but it provides good reason to believe that productivity has gone up in all of them.

It may well be true that productivity in the service and other omitted industries (taken as a group) has risen less rapidly than productivity in the industries for which there are good long-period statistics. If that is the case, we are underestimating the proportion of industries with low rates of productivity. But even in that case we can be reasonably sure that an increase in productivity, whether large or small, has been a general phenomenon.

What about the fact that the available long-term indexes (and the indexes we could add for the recent period to cover the service and other industries) relate to *groups* of industries? Undoubtedly the group indexes show less variation in rates of growth than indexes for more narrowly defined industries would show, because the index for a group—for example, food manufactures —is an *average* of the indexes for the industries that comprise the group—canned foods, bakery products, meat packing products, etc. This is confirmed by the estimates for those individual industries for which separate information on labor productivity is available. To continue with food manufactures, at one extreme is the fruit and vegetable canning and preserving industry, which multiplied its labor productivity ninefold during the first half of the century; at the other end is meat packing, with only a 30 percent increase over the half century; and close to the average of the entire food group is the corn products refining industry. Thus the available collection of indexes understates the degree of divergence.

But, then, what happens to our first finding—that all industries have experienced *some* rise in labor productivity (and also in total productivity)? Is it undermined by the more detailed evidence (mostly on labor productivity), which extends the range of variation? The evidence does reveal a few individual industries with downward long-term trends. However, these produce highly complex products that have improved in quality to a degree not caught by the output indexes. An example is locomotive manufacture. In fuel efficiency, tractive power, and other characteristics, locomotives have been improved enormously. If adequate account could be taken of such improvements in quality, the number of industries with declining trends in labor productivity would diminish and probably vanish entirely. This is why I said at the opening of this chapter that every industry for which a reasonably adequate index is available has experienced long-term growth in output per man-hour.

There is, indeed, another reason for believing that few, if any, industries have experienced *declining* labor productivity trends. An industry with such a decline, or

even with a slow rate of increase, would find itself con-
fronted with labor costs and probably also total costs
per unit rising at a rate greater than costs in other industries. Thus the industry would have to raise its price
in relation to the prices of competing products. This
would tend to "price it out of the market," and the industry would tend to vanish—that is, to be displaced by
cheaper domestic substitutes or foreign supplies of the
same commodity—and this might well happen even *before* its productivity had actually fallen.

Of course, many industries—particularly in mining
and agriculture, but probably also in local transportation—have experienced pressure *tending* to make labor
productivity decline. The need to drill deeper to get
oil or the delays of urban traffic are common enough
experiences. But tending to offset these unfavorable developments, and in all measured cases actually more
than offsetting them, are improvements in technology
and other factors making for higher efficiency.

A further word must be added on the accuracy of the
available indexes for individual industries. Even the
"solidly based" indexes are often less reliable than the
indexes for the economy at large. In part, the deficiency
arises from the diversity of sources from which the data
on output and input come, which causes discrepancies
in the matching of output and input. These and other
statistical errors tend to cancel out in the indexes for
the economy as a whole.

Different choices of data and of solutions to difficulties encountered in calculating the productivity indexes
can lead to rather different results, as has already been
pointed out. The steel industry provides an example
that was brought into the limelight in 1965.

A controversy arose over the steel industry's ability to raise wages without raising prices, and the President of the United States thereupon asked his Council of Economic Advisers to look into the matter. A crucial question (though not the only one) was the rate of increase in the steel industry's output per man-hour. According to the usual calculations of the Bureau of Labor Statistics available at the time, steel output per man-hour had risen at an average annual rate of 2.2 percent over the period 1959–64. The council felt it desirable, however, to adjust the B.L.S. figures for changes in operating rates, including those arising from the strike in 1959, because labor productivity tends to be abnormally low when output is small. The council therefore omitted the quarter years with unusually low operating rates. This adjustment raised the average rate of increase in output per man-hour from 2.2 percent to 3.3 percent, which cast quite a different light on the situation.

This did not close the matter. The steel companies then pointed out that quarters when operating rates were high because of anticipation of the strike or because of replenishment of inventories when the strike was over should also have been omitted. This would serve to push back the calculated rate of increase in output per man-hour.

I might add still another point of view, this one expressed in the position taken by the steelworkers' union a couple of years earlier. The union argued that the productivity index appropriate when the wages of their members are under consideration is output per hour worked by wage earners alone, not by all workers. Because the proportion of salaried workers had increased, even the C.E.A. index showed less of a rise than it would have under the union's definition.

A difficulty in measuring labor (and total) productivity changes in individual industries is created by inter-industry flows of materials, fuel, services, and semifabricated components. This is a rather technical point, but it is important and deserves a few paragraphs.

For an individual industry, output is generally measured on a gross basis: that is, output is the value (at base-period prices) of work done by labor and tangible capital on the goods and services supplied by other industries, plus the value (also at base-period prices) of these supplies from other industries. (Gross output in this sense is "grosser" than gross national product, which differs from net product only by the amount of depreciation and other capital consumption). Subtraction of these supplies from gross output to yield an index of net output (as is in effect done to get the index of gross national product) would solve the problem. But only a few attempts to measure the net output of individual industries have been made, and these (except for agriculture) must be viewed as still largely experimental.

That the resulting error is not always small is indicated by the figures for agriculture. The index of *gross* output per man-hour for this industry (1953 relative to 1899) is 330. The index of *net* output per man-hour for agriculture is 250.

Industries have generally become more specialized and many now purchase materials and services formerly produced on their own premises. Power used in manufacturing is an example. To the extent that this is true, indexes of net output per man-hour would—as in the case of agriculture—rise less rapidly than indexes of gross output per man-hour. On the other hand, there is evidence that more efficient use of materials, fuel, and the like, has made for savings of these per unit of output. This has been significant in certain industries—for example, electric power plants. For these industries, the index of productivity based on gross output would understate the rise in efficiency.

Connections of this sort between industries create difficulties for the statistician whose job it is to make productivity measurements. The interindustry connections also point to some of the sources of productivity increase and the means used to diffuse technology. These are of wider interest, but before we consider them, let us see how fluctuations in the rates of growth of the industry indexes of labor productivity compare with those in the national index.

The rates of growth in the indexes for individual industries or groups of industries are highly variable— much more so than those of the national productivity indexes.

One reason is that the random errors in the industry indexes are probably greater than the errors in the national indexes. But there are also greater "real" random changes in the productivity of individual industries due to weather, technological developments, change in tariffs, strikes, and other factors that affect different industries at different times and in different degrees. Also, the effects of business and longer cycles differ among industries, probably being greater in the industries that produce durable consumer and capital goods.

One of the most striking changes in the rate of

growth of labor productivity occurred in agriculture during the 1930's. The shift is especially interesting because farming is often thought of as typically characterized by a low rate of productivity growth. Diminishing returns as new marginal lands are brought into production or as the soil of old lands is exhausted and the supposed inability of agriculture to profit from the mass production methods applied in manufacturing have been offered to support this notion. The evidence on productivity is consistent with this belief—but only up to the 1930's. Since then, American farming has increased its productivity at an extraordinary rate, even more rapidly than manufacturing.

The great shift in the agricultural rate of productivity increase is also interesting because it runs contrary to another notion often held—that the productivity trends of individual industries may generally be expected to show retarded rates of growth. These expectations have some basis in fact, though less in the data on productivity (which are not available for industries in their youthful stages, when retardation in the rate of growth of productivity might be expected to be noticeable) than in the history of technology and the data on relative prices. The farming indexes are more consistent with acceleration, however, than with retardation. Very likely this may be an "exception" to what may be a reasonably valid "rule." There have been other exceptions, as in petroleum refining. But even if these *are* simply exceptions, the "rule" of retardation, like other generalizations, needs to be taken with a grain of salt.

The increase in national productivity reflects a *general* increase in efficiency and in capital per worker in different industries. But why a general rise? We shall want to explore the reason more thoroughly in later chapters, but some preliminary remarks may be made at this point.

The forces making for an increase in tangible and intangible capital per worker and in efficiency—the sources of increase in labor productivity—impinge on all industries (including government operations), not just on some of them.

Some of the forces operate through the markets for labor and capital. Thus when savings make tangible capital plentiful in relation to labor and the services of labor become more expensive than the services of tangible capital, this is felt throughout the economy. Businessmen everywhere, and even government officials, find it profitable or economical to increase the volume of tangible capital per worker. When educational levels rise as private expenditures on education are lifted by higher incomes and by expanded government support, the relative prices of high-quality labor tend to fall and all industries find it profitable to seek ways to put the improved labor to use.

Some of the forces operate through the markets for materials, supplies, and equipment. When firms learn to produce new, improved, or lower-cost materials, or fuel, power, or equipment, they make these available to their old customers and to every new customer they can add to their list. Often, in fact, customers request and assist suppliers to improve the materials, equipment, and other things they need. The automobile industry worked with the steel industry, for example, to get better steel sheets for auto bodies. In either case, improvements make for higher productivity. When technological developments—for example, mechanical power, ball-bearings, the electric motor and light, the telephone, packaging machinery, or plastics—are potentially versatile enough to be put to use in different industries, sooner or later the profit motive and competitive pressures see to it that they are in fact used in different industries. In all these industries, then, technology, wherever it may originate, helps to raise efficiency in the use of labor and capital. And it also adds to inducements to increase capital per worker and to use better educated workers, for many technological developments must be embodied in equipment or other tangible capital and must be operated by trained people.

Some of the forces making for an increase in labor productivity operate through the markets for knowledge. Not all knowledge needs to be embodied in materials or machines to flow from one industry to another or from university or government laboratory to industry. Engaged in the diffusion of knowledge are the individual firms and laboratories that produce the knowledge and the publishers, consulting firms, and governmental bureaus that make it their business to convey and adapt knowledge. Nor do industries that use the knowledge remain passive—they actively seek it. Many firms, even small ones, send their representatives to fairs, conventions, and scientific meetings, and not only to give the men a bit of a vacation.

Knowledge—of innovations in production processes, or marketing methods, or business organization—that initially appears to be of use only in a few industries may sooner or later be adapted to the peculiar conditions of other industries. The straight-line system that helped revolutionize the automobile industry in the early 1900's was suggested by methods already in successful use in Chicago meat-packing establishments. Its adaptation to motor car manufacture stimulated its

spread to many other industries, of which cotton gar-
ment manufacture is just one example.

Although the forces that make for an increase in labor
productivity operate broadly across the entire economy,
they affect different industries at different times and in
different degrees. All industries seek to substitute
cheaper capital for more expensive labor. But some, like
the steel industry, can do this more readily than others,
such as the barber shop. All industries seek to advance
their technology and improve their products, but most
must content themselves with the host of small innovations that crop up almost continuously over the full
range of economic life. The mechanical loom of today is
far better than the loom of fifty years ago, but it is not
fundamentally different. Some industries, however—
petroleum refining, with its "cracking" process, is an
example—do succeed in making large innovations.
Sometimes the innovations are revolutionary enough to
give birth to new industries so that the effects on productivity are not even reflected in the indexes of the old
industries in which the innovations originated. The syn-
thetic fibers industry, for example, was a small part of
the chemical industry before it broke away in 1923.

These observations lead to another conclusion worth
recording. It concerns the "credit" for an industry's
gain in productivity. It is true that what happens in an
industry is influenced by the diligence, enterprise, and
ability of its workers, management, and investors. It is
also true, however, that what happens is influenced, in
addition, by the quality and quantity of the materials,
machines, services, and ideas that the industry obtains
from other industries, both domestic and foreign. The
automobile industry was able to raise its productivity

because the steel industry supplied it with sheets that could be shaped more easily into body parts. And agriculture was able to raise its productivity because the automobile industry supplied it with versatile tractors, and still other industries supplied it with gasoline, fertilizers, pesticides, milking machines, and electric power. The credit for an industry's progress may often be claimed by one or another group, but it is seldom possible to back up the claim with good evidence.

Some things have already been said about the sources of higher productivity, but hardly enough. We therefore turn next to these, beginning with education and the other factors that raise the quality of labor.

PART II

Sources of Higher Productivity

PART II

Sources of Health Production

CHAPTER IV

Better Quality of Labor

"He that hath a trade hath an estate," was Ben Franklin's way of advising young men that training pays off. In more modern and more general language, we say that training and other efforts to improve the quality of labor constitute an investment in human capital that yields a return. Investment in human capital, like investment in tangible capital, is a source of higher labor productivity.

This has been recognized for a long time, as the quotation from "Poor Richard's Almanack" reminds us. Yet only in very recent years has the quality of labor received the attention it deserves in the plans and efforts the world is making to raise production. Shortly after the war, a United Nations committee set up to determine the capital requirements of the developing nations devoted its entire attention to tangible capital. It did not even mention the capital required for investment in human capital.

We would not make that blunder today. As a result of recent research, we have learned that the quality of labor contributes more to output than we had formerly realized. We have learned, also, that investment in education has been growing rapidly, and—in the United States, at least—may now be as large as investment in buildings and equipment. We can understand why East Germany, appalled by the flight of professional and skilled workers to the West, locked tight the escape hatch to West Berlin; and why Britain, not willing to stop emigration by force, worries about her "brains drain."

Human capital has become an element in every up-to-date development plan. The improvement in labor quality brought by investment in human capital is now an explicit variable in every modern effort to explain differences among countries in levels and rates of growth of productivity and output.

Just what is meant by quality of labor?

We say that one kind of labor is of better quality than another kind when—each kind of labor being applied in its appropriate context—a unit of the one adds more to production than a unit of the other. When one kind of labor is more productive than another kind, it will be more valuable. And when it is worth more, it will generally earn more. In fact, we can measure the quality of an hour of labor by its price or earnings, which tends to equal its value in production in a competitive market.

But why does one kind of labor yield more or less output than another kind? The difference depends on the strength, energy, and persistence with which workers apply themselves and on their knowledge, skill, and flexibility. If they get things done better and faster than others, if they are able to do useful things that other people cannot do at all, if they are better able to learn and unlearn and thus to adapt more readily to new methods, materials, machines, and products, if they can get along with less costly supervision—if they have any or all of these capacities, we count their labor as of better quality.

Any automobile service station provides an example. Drive your old car in and ask for a grease job, a change of oil, and a new oil filter. Were the "grease monkey" unable to read, he would not be able to go to the service manual and be sure of the points that require grease or oil and of the right size of filter. He would not be able to do as good a job as a literate person unless he had more supervision. He would be worth less, he would be paid less.

This does not necessarily mean that the more the worker in a job knows, the more he is worth in that job. A graduate automotive engineer would not be better at servicing a car than an alert gas station attendant and would not be worth more doing that kind of work. To judge the qualities of different kinds of labor, each kind must be applied in the job for which it is best suited. When he is appropriately used, the automotive engineer will have a greater value in production—will produce more and will receive more—than the "grease monkey."

When we talk about labor quality, the reader will notice, we are talking about a complex of characteristics, not a single characteristic that can be measured along one dimension. We say that a country's labor force is of better quality now than before when a weighted average of the various relevant characteristics of the labor force is greater now than before.

As in the measurement of national output, the weights assigned to the several kinds of labor quality are derived from their respective values or market prices in a base period. As in the case of output, also, different base periods will give different answers. The time of an average white-collar worker may be worth substantially more than that of a blue-collar worker, as it was before World War I, or it may be about the same, as it is today. The ratio changes as changes occur in the relative demand and supply of the different qualities of labor. The fact that there are proportionately more high-school graduates now than there were before World War I, for example, helps to explain the somewhat slower growth in white-collar salaries than in manual-worker wages.

But we can be sure that at all times and in all places the labor of a person who is quick to learn and has made the effort to learn will be of better quality and will command a higher wage or salary than the labor of a lazy dolt. Although we cannot avoid some ambiguity in talking about a better or worse quality of labor, the ambiguity is no more serious than it is when we talk about more or less national output. For most practical purposes we may ignore it.

It is easier to talk about measuring change in labor quality, however, than actually to measure it.

What we need, in principle, is a distribution of the labor force, or of the workers or man-hours employed, in each of the periods (or countries) to be compared, classified by detailed quality characteristics. These would be characteristics determined by objective criteria of intelligence, strength, knowledge, experience, etc. An example of a group in this multi-dimensional distribution would be the workers with something like the following set of characteristics: male, an I.Q. of 100–105, a high-school diploma, five to ten years of experience in a particular occupation, and good health. If, then, we knew what the average hourly earnings of the workers in each such group were in the base period, we would be able to see how much five points more of I.Q., a year more of education, two years more of experience —all other characteristics held constant—would yield in earnings. With this information we could calculate the weighted average change in the quality of all workers. If the number of workers of better quality had risen more than the number of workers of lesser quality, the average quality would be shown to have gone up.

Such detailed information is lacking. What economists have done, therefore, is to approximate the desired measurement of change in labor quality by using the limited information available. One such effort for the United States (by Edward F. Denison) makes use of information on three characteristics of the labor force that are associated with quality: age, sex, and length of formal education. Another (by John W. Kendrick) uses information on just one characteristic associated with quality of labor: the industry to which the worker is attached.

By either estimate, the rise in the average quality of labor has been substantial. But the two estimates differ, and it is therefore worth saying a little about them, so that we may better appreciate their precision or lack of precision. More important, this will also help us to understand better the factors that determine labor quality.

The first estimate of change in the average quality of labor starts with the well-known facts that earnings vary with age, sex, and education and that the age-sex-educational composition of the labor force has changed.

More specifically, we know that the earnings of the young of both sexes and of females of adult age are considerably below the earnings of adult males. Over the last fifty years or so, male and female workers under twenty years of age earned only about a third of what adult males earned, and adult females earned about 50 to 70 percent of the adult male wage. The reasons are pretty clear. Young people lack the experience that adult men have, and most women do not stick with an occupation long enough to reach the level of experience of men. Experience is not all of the story, but more detailed analysis indicates that the differences in earnings correspond reasonably well with differences in quality.

Because age is correlated with extent of education, the identification of age already makes some allowance for educational level. But differences in the education of adult workers still remain to be accounted for. According to the 1960 census, the average annual income of adult males of a given age, say forty, who were high-school graduates was about 35 percent above that of men of similar age but with only an elementary school education. Those who had completed college had an average income about 130 percent higher than eighth-grade graduates.

What happened to the proportions in the labor force of the young, of women, and of the educated? The relative number of young people under twenty declined as schooling was extended. This tended to *raise* the average quality of the labor force. The relative number of women twenty years of age and over rose as more and more of them left the household for short or long periods to take commercial employment. This tended to *reduce* the average quality of the labor force. Finally, educational levels rose as a larger and larger proportion of the workers acquired more education before they entered the labor force. Indeed, the average number of school years completed per person in the labor force rose by almost 60 percent between 1910 and 1960, and nearly as large an increase occurred in the average number of school days per school year completed. This larger investment in education tended to *raise* the average quality of the labor force.

What we know suggests that the two developments—more education and less child labor—tending to raise the average quality of labor were much more powerful than the development—more women in the labor force—tending to lower it. The net outcome was a rise in the quality of labor between 1910 and 1960 of something just under 60 percent, or 0.9 percent per annum.

This estimate may be on the high side. For one thing, a part of the income differences associated with education reflects innate ability and family position rather than more years of schooling. Also, it may be an exaggeration to assume, as the estimate does, that the lengthening of the school year has helped raise educational levels in exactly the same proportion. Further, the estimate fails to take account of informal training. Some of the growth of formal education, we should recognize, has merely displaced training on the job. Abe Lincoln read the law in his employer's office, while today's budding counselor starts by attending a law school. Informal training may also have grown but probably less rapidly than formal education. Similarly, a slower rate of growth may have also characterized the other sources of improved labor quality—health has been mentioned—that are omitted.

All this suggests that the correct figure for the rate of growth of labor quality is under 0.9 percent per year.

Kendrick

The alternative estimate of change in the average quality of labor assumes that differences between industries in average earnings of labor largely reflect corresponding differences between the industries in the quality of their labor.

Industrial differences in earnings are substantial. The average hourly earnings of farm workers, for example, are far below those of workers outside of agriculture, and textile workers earn less than workers in transportation equipment factories. Further, these earnings differentials appear to be fairly well correlated with corresponding differences among industries in such specific characteristics of their labor forces as age, sex, and education, when adequate comparisons are available. The assumption that the earnings differentials measure quality differentials is therefore reasonable, and we can legitimately use changes in the industrial distribution of employment to derive changes in the average quality of labor.

The shift in the industrial distribution of employment has on net balance been from lower to higher labor-earnings industries. The labor force attached to agriculture, just mentioned, has declined drastically, and employment in urban pursuits, in which average earnings are higher, has increased. And there have been shifts in the same direction within the urban labor force. The estimate of increase in the average quality of labor, made in this way, turns out to be 0.4 percent per annum over the period 1889–1960.

The estimate of 0.4 percent is only about half the estimate of 0.9 percent per annum. The fact that the 0.4 figure is derived from information covering a longer period than is the 0.9, may help to explain some of the difference, for there is some evidence that educational levels rose less rapidly before than after World War I. We have concluded, also, that the 0.9 percent is on the high side. But there are, in addition, some grounds for believing that the 0.4 percent is an underestimate.

One of the assumptions made in deriving the estimate of 0.4 percent is that all the labor *within* an industry is of unchanging quality. This assumption, forced by lack of adequate information, seems shaky. What information there is indicates that broad advances in education, health, and the like have improved the quality of labor within industries generally. The estimate of 0.4 percent takes no account of these intraindustry improvements in labor quality.

Probably the best estimate of the annual increase in average quality of labor between 1889 and 1960 falls somewhere between the two figures, 0.9 percent and 0.4 percent. We do not know just where, but we can be confident that the rise in the average quality of labor in the United States has been substantial.

An average annual rate of increase of something between 0.4 to 0.9 percent in the average quality of labor means that this factor can help significantly to explain the 2.4 percent average annual rate of increase in labor productivity.

Let us make an explicit calculation.

The increase in the quality of labor is, of course, an increase in only *one* of the *two* main groups of inputs that affect labor productivity. Since *total* input also includes tangible capital, the improvement in the quality of labor would raise it by less than the 0.4 to 0.9 percent. By how much less? That depends on the relative importance of labor in total input. The relative importance of labor is measured by the fraction of national income going to labor, a fraction that has ranged between .7 and .8. The contribution of improved labor quality to the average annual percentage increase in labor productivity is, then, about three quarters of 0.4 to 0.9, that is, 0.3 to 0.7. Assuming the correct figure to be about halfway between these limits, we may conclude as follows: Improved labor quality contributed 0.5 out of 2.4 or as much as 20 percent of the average annual rate of increase in labor productivity.

Investment in education raises labor productivity. It does not necessarily follow, however, that the more investment in education the better. Alternative sources of an increase in labor productivity, such as investment in tangible capital, may be even more profitable. Only if a dollar devoted to education would yield a greater rate of return than would its alternative uses, may we speak of underinvestment in education.

The question of under- or overinvestment in education arises whenever local school budgets and federal government support of education are discussed. The question arises also, or should arise, when private expenditures on education are contemplated. To help answer the question, which is part of the general question of proper balance in investment, we turn to estimates of the percentage rates of return on investment in education. These were calculated as one would calculate a rate of return on a bond or an investment in a factory.

The rate of return on an investment in college education in this country, as the student and his family would see it from their private point of view, takes into account only the costs borne by them and the returns received by them.

The costs include not only the out-of-pocket expenditures on fees and extra living costs with which we are all familiar. Included also, and usually more important, is the income that the student forgoes by going to school instead of to work. The sum of these private costs incurred by the time of graduation from college, plus the interest on the investment to that date, may be said to be the cost of the investment.

The returns on the investment are measured by the differences between the after-tax incomes of college graduates and high-school graduates in each year following the date of graduation from high school. The difference in income will be in favor of high-school graduates during the four college years and probably also for a few years thereafter. In all the remaining forty-odd years of their working lives, however, the income differentials will be in favor of the college men. Because the income differentials are spread over time, they can be totaled and compared with the cost of investment only after discounting each year's differential back to the date of graduation from college.

The rate of discount that makes the present value of the income differentials equal to the present value of the costs, both calculated as of the date of graduation from college, is the rate of return on a college education.

The private yield so calculated (by Gary S. Becker)

was over 10 percent and perhaps as high as 12 or 14 percent in 1960. This estimate will be overstated because, as I mentioned earlier, the earnings of many college-trained men may reflect not only more education but also greater innate ability and better family connections. But even after allowance for these other factors, the estimate of the rate of return on a college education is of the same order of magnitude as the corresponding rate of return on ordinary business investments in manufacturing enterprises.

Private rates of return on a high-school education in the United States, similarly calculated, appear to be at least as high as the corresponding rates on a college education. This is true also of the rate of return on an elementary school education.

These rates of return provide good reasons (to which may be added other good reasons, noneconomic in character) why virtually all children in this country—99 percent of those aged seven to thirteen—now attend elementary school, and almost as large a fraction—93 percent of those aged fourteen to seventeen—now attend high school. The fraction in college is not as high. It is about a third or a fourth of those aged eighteen to twenty-two. On the basis of those proportions, one might expect that the rate of return on a college education would be much higher than the rate of return on an elementary or high school education. But the costs of a college education are much greater. The cost of a primary or secondary school education is very small to the student and his family, for public schools, to which most students go, charge no fees, and the earnings forgone under age fourteen or even eighteen would be very modest.

Obviously, many more teenagers could be going to college and staying through to commencement. However, since the rate of return on a college education is about the same as the rate of return on investment in manufacturing, from the strictly private (and strictly economic) viewpoint, increased investment in a college education does not appear to be more profitable than investment in other forms of capital. In other words, the available information provides no ground for believing that private investment in college education is either grossly insufficient or grossly excessive. The conclusion applies, however, only on the *average*. Not everyone who would profit economically or otherwise from a college education is able to command the funds needed to go to college. Nor should everybody now in college be there.

To assess the contribution of education to productivity and economic growth, particularly when the question is how much to expand public support of education, the relevant rate of return is the *social* rate of return. In the United States a great deal of the cost of education is borne by the government and philanthropic institutions. Social costs—essentially private and public costs combined—therefore greatly exceed private costs.

But it is also the case that social benefits exceed private benefits. Private earnings from education are measured after deducting income taxes, and social earnings are measured before those deductions. In addition, certain benefits reach society as a whole for which no compensation, or no commensurate compensation, is paid the college-trained or other educated person. One such benefit is rapid scientific and technological advance, which is more likely to take place when a larger number of persons have had a higher education.

To the extent that there are such social benefits—and there is little doubt that there are some—part of the increase in labor productivity that we have credited to greater efficiency belongs instead to the credit of better labor quality. The estimates previously cited understate the contribution of the increase in labor quality. If society as a whole would benefit greatly from having many more college-trained men and women than there now are, as many people agree, the social rate of return on investment in college training may be well in excess of 10, 12, or 14 percent.

The reader will recall that virtually every industry in the United States increased its labor productivity over the years. One reason is the well-nigh universal improvement that has taken place in the quality of labor.

Consider the simple fact of reduction in illiteracy. In 1870, over 20 percent of the population of ten and over was illiterate. By 1960, the rate was down to only 2 percent of the population fourteen and over. Beyond that, of course, is the growing fraction of persons who have completed high school or college. An increase in this fraction is visible in the employment records of industries throughout the economy.

As we might expect, however, the rate of improvement in the quality of labor has been larger in some industries than in others. Along with other reasons, this difference explains why labor productivity in some industries rose more rapidly than productivity in other industries.

Hardly any reference has been made to food and health in discussing the improved quality of labor in the United States. There is no doubt that the amount and kind of food and the conditions of living and working and playing affect the strength, health, and stamina of the labor force. At one time a section of the Pan American Highway running through Central America was referred to as "the road that food built" when it was found that supplementing the prevailing sugar-cane diet of the road workers with protein foods led to substantial gains in the work done. We can be sure that this factor is significant in explaining international differences in labor productivity.

In the United States, however, the effect on labor quality of changes in health and vigor seems to have been small. The problems of inadequate food and parasitic disease, for example, so serious in the poorer countries of the world, have never been nearly as important in this country.

This is not to say that improvement in the health of the average worker in this country has been lacking. We know that many fewer southern workers, for example, are now subject to the debilitating effects of hookworm, from which they suffered severely only two or three generations ago. We know also that this improvement in health must have helped raise labor productivity. But we have only vague ideas of the general rate of improvement in health, and of its contribution to the rise in labor productivity.

CHAPTER V

More Tangible Capital

For a long time now, man has been defined as "the tool-using animal." In line with this emphasis on men's use of tools, more tangible capital has been considered the dominant cause of the increase in labor productivity.

We now realize that an increase in the intangible capital invested in human beings, of the sort discussed in the preceding chapter, and an increase in efficiency due to technological change and other factors, to be discussed in the following chapter, are not less important and not less reliable than tangible capital as sources of increased labor productivity.

But although tangible capital is not so overwhelmingly important as had formerly been supposed, it is nevertheless of vital importance. The highly trained labor of the United States is used effectively because it has more and better tangible capital goods with which to work. And many of the country's technological advances reach the stage of application because we are able to embody them in capital goods.

Without the $2 trillion of plant and equipment, rolling stock and inventories, land and roads, dams and water systems, mines and quarries, and the other forms of tangible capital goods that we counted in our national wealth in 1964, the nation's labor productivity could not be what it is.

Two trillion dollars of tangible capital goods sounds like a lot of capital goods, and the reader may wonder if the figure is inflated. It is not. The nation's stock of tangible capital is measured net of accumulated depreciation and obsolescence. This means that all except the very newest capital goods of the country are counted in the total at less than current or replacement cost; and obsolete plant and equipment that *could* be used, but which, except as standby facilities it no longer pays to use, are counted at no more than scrap value.

But why, one may ask, should land and minerals and other subsoil assets be included in the national wealth? "Natural resources cost nothing." In fact, however, many so-called natural resources are not natural. They are produced by men, and they do cost something. A great deal of our farmland was made by men working hard to remove the forest cover and to drain and irrigate the soil. Oilwells and gaswells are continually being produced by investment in the search for "gushers" and in their development once they have been discovered. But even if these forms of capital had cost us nothing, they would make production higher than it would otherwise be and would belong in our list of sources of higher productivity. Some valuable natural resources, such as the waterways provided by the Great Lakes, cost nothing and for that reason are excluded from the national wealth. Yet without these natural waterways the costs of transporting heavy ores, coal, and stone in the Middle West would have been far higher than they were, and our steel industry could not have developed as well or as rapidly as it did.

A different question might be raised about business inventories, which accounted for over $150 billion of the total in 1964. An economist with whom I once discussed the role of capital in raising labor productivity surprised me by asking what inventories do. "Don't they just sit there? Can they save labor, like machines?" They can and do. By "sitting" there, ready when needed, inventories do save labor. Inventories of raw materials eliminate the need to run back and forth to get supplies. Any housewife who has profited from her husband's gift of a deep freeze knows how much shopping time and trouble it saves her. Inventories of partially finished goods, used as needed, make it possible to turn out large batches at lower cost. And inventories of finished products, stocked as "shelf" goods, help stabilize production and keep costs down even when sales fluctuate. Like plant and equipment, then, inventories help make labor productivity higher than it would otherwise be.

Rather than being inflated, the $2 trillion is a conservative figure, for it excludes not only the natural waterways, but also several other major items of capital. One such excluded item is the great volume of family-owned consumer equipment, with a net value of over $250 billion. Another large item that is excluded is the military equipment held by the federal government. Consumer equipment and military equipment are excluded from the conventional measurement of national wealth, just as their services are excluded from the conventional measurement of national product. Under different accounting conventions, they would be taken into account when measuring output and capital, and the totals would be raised accordingly.

With seventy million persons employed in civilian occupations in 1964, $2 trillion worth of national capital provided the average worker with the collaboration of close to $30,000 worth of tangible capital.

The amount of tangible capital per worker in particular industries ranged widely around the $30,000 average. An example of a high figure—six times the average for manufacturing industry as a whole—is provided by the petroleum refining industry. A visitor to a petroleum "cracking" plant would be impressed, first, by the vast array of connected pipes and tanks, which seems to have been designed by a super-Rube Goldberg, and, second, by the few people he would see working around the plant. The same eerie feeling of machinery spinning around by itself crawls up one's spine in an electric-power plant or an electronic computer room.

Of course, these industries are exceptional. There are many industries in which capital per worker runs to much less than $30,000. Very few, however, fail to provide each worker with hundreds if not thousands of dollars worth of tools, equipment, supplies, and working space. Even the "Good Humor" man now peddles his ice cream from a motor truck containing a built-in refrigerator. And the barber no longer works up a lather by hand.

A most striking example of the extent to which

tangible capital had been given the work formerly done by human hands—in farming, surprisingly enough—was reported in the newspapers a few years ago when a boy playing around with a .22 rifle shot off some of the insulators supporting the high tension wires crossing the Cape Cod Canal. All the electricity on the Cape was knocked out for many hours, and cows moaned with pain because they could not be milked. There simply were no longer enough people left on the cape's farms to take over and do the milking by hand when the electric milkers shut off—even had all the farmers and their families still retained the skill, which was not the case.

The existing stock of tangible capital represents the accumulation of every year in our history, except the few periods of very deep depression, when the value of new capital goods added to the stock fell below the value lost by wear and tear, obsolescence, and the scrapping of old capital goods. Naturally, the total capital accumulated over years cannot be expressed in the original prices prevailing in each of these years if the total is to be meaningful. Therefore, we have to make an adjustment for changes in prices. The 1964 total that I cited is the sum of the value of the capital goods added at various times (less depreciation and obsolescence), with all the values calculated at prices prevailing in 1964.

Expressed in these "constant" 1964 prices—what economists call "real terms"—the net tangible capital assets of the United States today are over six times what they were in 1889. The number of workers also increased, but at a slower rate, and hours per man fell, so that man-hours little more than doubled. Tangible capital per man-hour, therefore, is now about three times what it was toward the end of the nineteenth century. This suggests that the increase in tangible capital per man-hour contributed significantly to the rise in output per man-hour.

It is interesting to note that the average rate of increase in tangible capital per man-hour was somewhat higher between 1889 and the 1920's than during the period since. It was about 1.6 percent per annum in the earlier period and 1.3 percent in the recent period. Contrast this with the fact we learned in Chapter II, namely, that labor productivity rose less rapidly during the earlier than during the more recent period. This comparison suggests a rather considerable decline in the relative importance of tangible capital per man-hour as a source of increase in labor productivity. We will have more to say about this in a moment.

The tripling of tangible capital per man-hour in the economy at large is, of course, an average of the corresponding rates of increase in the individual industries that make up the whole economy.

As we would expect, about half the industries of the country multiplied capital per man-hour by more than three times over the past three quarters of a century. Unusually large increases were experienced in processed tobacco products, petroleum refining, the natural gas industry, some branches of transportation, bituminous coal mining, and rubber manufactures.

In the pre-World War I tobacco industry, for example, cigar manufacture was entirely a hand process. Then, in the 1920's, there appeared the machine-made cigar, promoted by an intensive advertising campaign on the horrors of the spit used by some cigar makers in rolling handmade cigars. Today, even high-quality cigars are mostly machine-made.

Coal mining provides another example. It was essentially a pick and shovel operation in the early days. In present-day coal mines a large investment in elaborate machines has lightened the human burden of cutting, loading, and conveying the coal from below ground to the surface. In addition, open-pit mining has been displacing the underground mines as the power shovels used to strip away the surface cover of earth have grown bigger and bigger. By 1960, the largest shovel in use had reached a capacity of as much as eighty-five cubic yards. It is already more than double that today, with the bucket big enough to scoop up, with one bite, not only the contents of several large dump trucks but the trucks themselves.

Just as half the industries of the country have increased their tangible capital per man-hour by more than the overall average, half have increased it by less. Few industries, however, have failed to supply their workers with more tangible capital. The few with a decline in tangible capital per man-hour are primarily those that have been growing very slowly, or even declining, such as local electric railways. In the circumstances, these industries have been able to get along with a gradually depreciating stock of old capital equipment. The "constant-price" net value of this capital has thus fallen more than have man-hours of employment.

By substituting tangible capital for labor—cigar machines for hand-rolling or mechanical coal-cutters and loaders for men with picks and shovels—increases in tangible capital per man-hour have helped raise output per man-hour.

Let us be more specific: How much did the tripling of tangible capital per man-hour since 1889 (a rise equal to 1.5 percent per year) contribute to the quintupling of output per man-hour (a rise equal to 2.4 percent per year)?

What we are asking is essentially this: By how much would output per man-hour increase if tangible capital per man-hour, and only tangible capital per man-hour, were to increase by 1.5 percent—that is, if the change in capital per man-hour were accompanied by no change in the quality of labor and in efficiency?

We know that a given percentage increase in tangible capital per man-hour when that is the only source of change in labor productivity cannot lead to an equal percentage increase in labor productivity. Its contribution depends on the relative importance of tangible capital in total input, and this importance is measured by the fraction of national income paid for the services of tangible capital. The fraction, equal to about 0.2 or 0.3, is the complement of the fraction measuring the relative importance of labor's services, which is between 0.7 and 0.8. A 1 percent increase in tangible capital per man-hour may be expected, then, to raise output per man-hour by about a quarter of 1 percent. And the 1.5 percent per year increase that actually took place in tangible capital per man-hour, we may estimate, on this basis, accounted for about 0.4, or a sixth, of the 2.4 percent per year increase in labor productivity.

In industries in which tangible capital per man-hour rose more rapidly than 1.5 percent per annum and in which tangible capital accounted for more than 25 percent of total input, the contribution of the rise in tangible capital per man-hour must have exceeded 0.4 percentage points. In industries below the average in both respects, the contribution must have been less than 0.4 percentage points. In industries that were above average in respect of one quantity but below average in respect of the other, how much the rise in tangible capital per man-hour contributed would depend on the product of the two quantities. The effect on labor productivity even of a very high rate of increase in tangible capital per man-hour, for example, must be modest when tangible capital is of small importance relative to labor. Providing a barber with two razors instead of one will save him some time and raise his productivity—but not by much.

To return to the economy as a whole, we have seen that tangible capital per worker rose more rapidly during the first half than during the second half of the eighty years or so since 1889. Also, the relative importance of tangible capital was somewhat higher in the earlier than in the later period. It follows that tangible capital per man-hour contributed more to the increase in labor productivity in the earlier period than in the later period. Further, since labor productivity increased less rapidly in the earlier period, the *relative* contribution of increased tangible capital per man-hour was greater still. Indeed, it was about a fifth, as compared with about a tenth in the more recent period. Factors other than tangible capital grew in relative importance.

The reader will remember that total tangible capital grew less rapidly than total output—about 2.5 percent per annum for capital as against 3.5 for output. The long-term trend in the ratio of capital to output has therefore been downward, declining about 1 percent per annum. By 1964, in fact, it required only half as much tangible capital to turn out a unit of product as it did in 1889; in other words, the productivity of tangible capital had doubled.

This interesting change in the relation between capital and output deserves a few more words because some people, even some economists, believe that a unit of national output requires the use of a set amount of tangible capital. They take it for granted, in other words, that the national "capital-output ratio" (as the relation between tangible capital and output is expressed in development programs) is rather constant over time. This has not been the case in the United States, nor in other countries.

Stability in the capital-output ratio runs contrary not only to our experience but also to what we might sensibly expect from our knowledge of economic behavior. Powerful forces from all directions push on the capital-output ratio. It would be surprising indeed if they just happened to balance one another.

One force originates in the great increase in tangible capital made possible by personal, corporate, and governmental saving. The resulting rise in tangible capital per worker has tended to reduce the price—or "rental value"—of the services of capital goods relative to the price of labor's services. In turn, the relative cheapening of tangible capital's services has induced businessmen to substitute tangible capital for labor. It thus became profitable to add proportionately more tangible capital than labor when output expanded. When the volume of materials to be handled increased, for example, the need was met by employing more fork trucks rather than laborers. This substitution has tended to increase the capital-output ratio.

On the other hand, a second group of factors—technological change and the other factors that make for increases in efficiency—has also been at work. These have tended to reduce the amount of capital, as well as labor, used per unit of product. By cutting the time for making steel from hours to minutes, for example, the "basic oxygen" process has radically reduced the investment required per ton of steel produced.

The net outcome of these opposing tendencies could have been a rise or a fall or—if "the coin stood on its edge"—even stability in the national capital-output ratio. The statistics tell us that it was a decline. The capital-saving tendency of improved efficiency has been more powerful than the capital-raising tendency resulting from the substitution of capital for labor.

The estimates of the contribution of tangible capital per man-hour to the growth of labor productivity may seem to some readers to be surprisingly low. They may wonder whether we are not underestimating the contribution of capital by ignoring the link between technological progress and growth in tangible capital. Could we have very much technological advance without growth of capital? Is not a good deal of the technological change "embodied" in tangible capital, as mentioned at the beginning of this chapter? These are good questions, for they point to the limitations of our measurements.

When we speak of the contribution of tangible capital, we are thinking only of the services rendered by those who built the equipment or other tangible capital goods and by the savers who were willing to finance the capital goods by making some of their money available for this purpose. We are not thinking of the changing form the capital goods may take as a result of technological advance or of the services of those who contributed to technological advance.

Capital goods—and men also—do improve as technology advances, and these improvements do help raise labor productivity. But we count the contribution of these improvements under the heading of technological change and include it in our measurement of the contribution of improved efficiency.

There is little else we can do in the present state of our knowledge. The question of "embodiment" serves, however, to remind us that our classification of the factors that play a part in labor productivity slurs over important interrelationships among them. Consider the following:

1. Better trained labor makes it possible to use more and better capital efficiently. Imagine an illiterate trying to run a computer!
2. More and better capital makes it possible to use highly trained labor efficiently. Professionals leave their countries when they find they cannot get the sophisticated and expensive equipment they need at home, and a "brains drain" results.
3. More capital makes it possible to apply advanced technologies. A modern steel rolling mill cannot be run without a heavy investment in controls.
4. Improved technologies make it possible to employ more

capital effectively. The mechanical shovels used in strip mining, described earlier, would not be as big, and as efficient, had not technology made them possible.

In a word, capital, labor, technological change, and the other factors that play a part in production are complements: they "need" one another.

CHAPTER VI

Greater Efficiency in the Use of Labor and Capital

Of the three sources of increased output per man-hour in the United States—better quality of labor, more tangible capital, and greater efficiency in the use of labor and tangible capital—it is the last that bulks largest.

Over the past three quarters of a century, we saw in Chapter IV, better quality of labor contributed about a half a percentage point, or a bit more, to the annual rate of growth of labor productivity. And in Chapter V, we found that an increase in tangible capital per man-hour contributed just under another half percentage point. In round numbers, then, these two sources together yielded about one percentage point. What is left —the larger part—is the difference between this percentage point and the approximately two and a half percentage points that measure the average annual rate of increase in labor productivity. This difference of about one and a half percentage points—1.7 percent per annum, to be exact—measures the rate of increase of efficiency in the utilization of labor and capital.

The figure is the same as that obtained in Chapter II, when we calculated the rate of increase in output per unit of labor and tangible capital combined. This is because the calculations are essentially the same. They differ merely in the order of the several steps in the calculations.

This increase in efficiency has been a source of the increase in labor productivity not only "on the average" but in every industry for which there are records, as we saw in Chapter III. Indeed, the increase in efficiency was the *major* source of higher labor productivity in most industries. Even though improved labor quality contributed significantly in most industries and so did more tangible capital per man-hour, the sum of these contributions was generally less than the contribution of greater efficiency.

Why did efficiency improve? Technological change has been mentioned several times, but it is not the only factor, despite the habit some economists have of treating a change in efficiency and a change in technology as synonymous. Technological change, yes; but what else?

There are, in fact, many determinants of efficiency. Besides technology there are other kinds of useful knowledge, which most of us would not think of as "technological." There is also the size of the market, which can permit or limit the specialization of workers, machines, and business establishments. Prevailing hours of labor also can affect the pace and thus the efficiency of work done. And there are, in addition, the many and diverse elements of a country's economic organization and policy and its political and cultural heritage. These, which can assist or can obstruct the efficient allocation of the country's resources among alternative uses, range from agricultural policy to the treatment of minority groups of the population. There are, in fact, so many determinants of efficiency that it is necessary to arrange them in groups, as we have done, if we are not to be lost in a jungle of factors.

Economists have learned a good deal about the identity of these factors and the ways in which they influence efficiency, which deserve our attention. As we shall see, however, we shall not be able to be as definite as before about quantitative effects.

The first group of determinants of efficiency that we identify embraces all kinds of useful knowledge. Since we exclude the *diffusion* of existing knowledge through formal and informal education, which we have already taken into account under the heading of "quality of labor," it is *new* knowledge that we are concerned with here—the knowledge that results when new products, materials, or techniques of production are invented, discovered, or adapted to wider uses.

In an age of spectacular technological advance, in which thousands of people fly across the Atlantic every day and many more thousands work in what are called push-button factories, it is hardly necessary to argue that a growth of knowledge has helped raise efficiency and thereby labor productivity also.

What we must stress is, first, that the advances in technology that raise efficiency from one year to another consist of more than "technological breakthroughs." In addition to the fundamental new ideas, there are a host of modest improvements that, over many years, follow the breakthroughs and turn them from interesting ideas written up in the Sunday supplements into economically significant facts. Indeed, between any pair of years it is the large number of prosaic changes, rather than the spectacular developments, that account for the bulk of the rise in efficiency. This is indicated by the more or less continuous rise in national efficiency described in Chapter II and by the well-nigh universal increase in the efficiency of the various industries of the United States observed in Chapter III.

The importance of modest improvements is indicated also by the history of technology. The invention of the steam engine did not raise efficiency over night. It took years to develop the basic idea and bring it to the point where it could enter the market. Had not James Watt found a partner in Matthew Boulton who had both faith in the idea and the money to finance the long work of "research and development," the engine might not have become a serious commercial possibility in Watt's lifetime. And once the steam engine did begin to sell, it took many more years of effort by Boulton and Watt, and then by other inventors, engineers, and business-men, to widen its market. Fuel requirements had to be lowered, weight reduced, and reliability increased by combing out "bugs" before the engine could find uses in various mining and manufacturing industries and begin to revolutionize ocean and land transportation.

An example closer to home is the automobile. Its market would not be what it is today had not the fre-quent need to "get out and get under" been eliminated, the self-starter invented, flats and blowouts become rar-ities, and crossing the Rockies turned from an adventure for hardy souls into a pleasurable excursion. All this took years and years.

Since I have mentioned the automobile, let me refer

also to the petroleum refining industry, which has been among the leaders in increasing efficiency. The old method of refining oil involved a distillation process much like the distillation of liquor or alcohol from wine or mash. The lighter products that came in the first "runnings," essentially gasoline, were useless and even dangerous. Not until automobile demand appeared near the turn of the century was there any market for the gasoline, and not until automobiles had grown in number did the demand for gasoline begin to outrun the supply provided by the distillation process. And only then, around 1913, did the refining method that is now dominant—the "cracking" process—become commercially successful. Yet the first patents for cracking date back to the 1880's, over a quarter century earlier. The establishment of the cracking process in 1913 did not end the story. Production had to be shut down frequently in order to clean out the cracking retort, and the process had other limitations. These were removed by a series of major (and many minor) improvements extending to the present day. The whole series of innovations, not just the initial breakthrough, explains the continuous and rapid rise in petroleum refining efficiency.

The second point worth stressing is that the advance of knowledge includes more than technology, if one accepts the narrow dictionary definition of technology as "the industrial arts." Some of the new knowledge that raises efficiency consists of improvements also in the "management arts." Not only the steam engine and the petroleum cracking process, in other words, but also time and motion study and the line system of factory production served to raise efficiency. Frederick Taylor and the other men who first thought of analyzing the production process with time and motion studies and the countless others who devised better ways of moving materials and parts along an assembly line contributed to the knowledge that raises productivity. To go further back, it has been said that logarithms doubled the lifetime of astronomers; and the rest of us save time by using checks to make payments and Arabic numbers to write out the amounts and balance our checkbooks.

A third point concerns the pace of technological advance, about which there is much talk these days. There are good reasons for believing that technological advance has been unusually rapid in our generation. Growth of knowledge and of productivity is a cumulative process that feeds on itself. The knowledge, trained people, and equipment needed to devise new technologies become available in greater supply. Economic growth also pushes up the demand for new products, materials, and methods and in this way, too, stimulates invention and innovation. The "mysterious coincidence" of similar inventions made almost simultaneously by different people reflects this concurrence of the conditions, on both the supply and demand sides, under which inventions take place.

It would be nice to be able to measure technological advance and demonstrate its speedier pace during our generation. But hard quantitative facts are scarce. The faster rate of increase in output per man-hour since the 1920's has frequently been cited to justify the belief that technological change has speeded up. But the index of labor productivity can hardly be said to reflect the advance of knowledge or technology alone, as I have been trying to explain. Another measure of technological change, number of patents, is suspect because patents may cover large developments in the useful arts or only small improvements, and in any case the number of patents is significantly affected by the cost of filing. Acceptance of the validity of patents as a measure of technological change diminished greatly when it was found that the rate of growth in the number of patents had declined in recent decades. Most frequently cited, now that the information is currently collected, are expenditures on research and development. These do show rapid advance in recent decades, but even they are unsatisfactory because they measure not technological change, but the costs incurred in certain, but not all, the "knowledge-producing industries." R. and D. expenditures do not measure the *output* of knowledge or —what we really have in mind when we talk about the pace of technological advance—the rate of increase in the *stock* of knowledge.

The fact that some part, and probably an increasing proportion, of the advance of knowledge is the result of deliberate investment that is made for the economic return that it may yield reminds us of another point referred to briefly in an earlier chapter. Investments in research and development could properly be classified under this heading of "more capital" rather than "greater efficiency." By failing to classify them in this way, are we not understating the contribution of capital to labor productivity and overstating the contribution of efficiency? The answer is not clear. Understatement of the contribution of capital and overstatement of the rise in efficiency will occur if the rate of increase in the services rendered by the stock of knowledge is more rapid than the rate of increase in the services rendered by the stock of tangible capital. This may be so, but we do not know whether it is so. We can only guess at the rate of increase in the services rendered by the stock of knowledge. If there is a misclassification of the factors that determine labor productivity, it is not a serious matter, however, so long as we can identify and distinguish the various factors in each class.

Just as economic growth generates further growth by stimulating the expansion of knowledge, it also paves the way for further growth by increasing the scale of economic activity. This is what Adam Smith had in mind long ago when he said in his *Wealth of Nations* that the "division of labor is limited by the extent of the market."

A larger market makes it possible to benefit from greater specialization not only of labor but also of tools and machines. A modern example, which explains why so few countries produce automobiles, is the radical reduction that occurs in the cost of making automobile engines, bodies, and parts when the volume of production expands and specialized dies, presses, and tools can be used economically. Establishments, firms, and industries can also become specialized, as anyone consulting the "yellow pages" of a large city's telephone directory can see.

What this comes down to is that nations can profit from being large. Large size does not itself *create* economies, but it *permits* the realization of whatever "economies of scale" are possible when markets are big and specialization can be carried far.

As a nation grows in population and production, an offset to the advantages yielded by greater specialization results from the pressure that growth puts on limited land, water, and other natural resources. But these "diminishing returns" do not yet appear to have been important in this country. Most economists believe the

United States to be highly productive, in part, because it is large.

The scale economies that are possible at any given time depend on the technology of the time. For example, a large nation can specialize little more than a small nation and gain little of the advantage of higher efficiency from its size when transport is by oxcart rather than steam railroad. As this example suggests, the possibilities of scale economies are also limited by the volume of tangible capital available for replacing oxcarts with railroads.

Also relevant are the obstacles to domestic and foreign commerce that may be imposed by tariffs, quotas, and other governmental regulations. When international trade is reasonably free, even a small nation can gain economies of scale by specializing in some kinds of production and selling in foreign markets the output it does not need for itself. What is really crucial is not the size of the nation but the size of the market. The Swiss watch industry is an excellent example of how producers even in a small country and consumers everywhere can gain from economies of scale.

Within countries, also, economies of scale may be limited because the free choice of type and size of industrial unit is restricted by various governmental regulations. When anti-chain-store legislation or other regulations inhibit the establishment of large and efficient enterprise (without appreciably improving fair competition), productivity is adversely affected.

Economists have spent a good deal of time trying to measure the economies of scale, but it is extremely difficult to distinguish between the economies that arise from increasing scale and the benefits that arise from technological progress. Except with regard to the relation between efficiency and size of establishment or enterprise, perhaps, economists have had little success in measuring economies of scale. In a special meeting of the International Economic Association held in 1957—precisely in order to assess "the economic consequences of the size of the nations"—the participants could agree that scale is important, but they could not agree on just how important it is.

The average hours of labor per worker fell in the United States from about fifty-three or fifty-four per week in 1889 to the present level of a trifle under forty. This also helped to raise efficiency.

When hours are long, the pace of work is slow, illness on the job is more frequent, accident rates are higher, and the proportion of spoiled products, of materials wasted, and of machines put out of order is above normal. Many studies have provided fairly clear evidence on this effect of long working hours, and it is reasonable to accept it as a fact. Just how much the reduction in hours has raised efficiency is not so clear, however, though much was claimed during the movement for the shorter workday.

A remarkable brief on the effect of shorter hours prepared by Felix Frankfurter and Josephine Goldmark, under the direction of Louis Brandeis, illustrates the kind of evidence available when the campaign was under way. The brief offered to the U.S. Supreme Court in 1915 in defense of the Oregon "Ten Hour Law" is famous for the number and variety of its citations. But the evidence it contained on the effect of changes in hours of work, like most of the evidence available even now, was not free of the effects of other factors. Whenever hours were reduced, a close reading of the evidence suggests, something else also was almost always changed. New equipment was installed, the plant was reorganized, labor incentives were improved, or new management came on the scene. The changes in productivity that followed changes in hours per worker reflected these changes also, not just the effects of reductions in hours.

During the period between 1889 and the 1920's, hours fell from over fifty-three per week per person to forty-nine. During the period since the 1920's, hours fell from forty-nine to just under forty. Does this mean that the contribution of the reduction in hours to the increase in efficiency was greater in the more recent period? Not necessarily. It is reasonable to suppose that the reduction of an hour in the length of the workweek would have a greater effect on efficiency when the reduction is from a high than from a low level. If so, it is possible that the five-and-a-half-hour reduction between 1889 and the 1920's contributed almost as much, or even as much, as the nine-hour reduction since. But this is largely surmise. We can be reasonably sure only that shortened hours contributed something significant in both periods.

I have left for the last the large group of institutional and cultural factors that have been identified as impeding or encouraging the optimum use of resources.

These include the great variety of policies followed in this and other countries that tend to support a larger agricultural, maritime, or oil industry than is economically (or even militarily) sensible when foreign supplies or facilities are available at low cost; policies to maintain so-called "fair-trade" prices, which keep inefficient stores in existence; obstacles to the introduction of new technologies imposed by industry, labor, and sometimes also government in order to protect existing investments and jobs, but which also prevent productivity from rising; policies to weaken competition by relaxing the enforcement of antitrust laws; restrictions on the consolidation of regulated industries, which have to forgo the benefits they could get by consolidation; discrimination on account of race, color, or sex, which lessens efficiency in many ways; and still others.

What is important for *change* in efficiency is, of course, the degree of *change* in these various factors, not their strength at any given time. Neither the United States, nor any other country has ever reached anything that may be called an optimum use of its resources. Our question is whether we have gotten closer to or further away from the optimum. Since some of the changes in a policy have made for greater efficiency and some for less, it is the *net* balance among the changes that counts.

The great variety of factors, the different directions and diverse ways in which they exert their influence, and their interrelations with other factors (already mentioned more than once in this chapter) make extremely hazardous any assessment of their net effect or of the separate effect of each. There is some ground for believing, however, that during the 1930's the passage of "protective" legislature on tariffs, agriculture, labor unions, and small retail trade carried the country further away from an optimum use of its resources. More recently, the shift seems to have been in the opposite direction.

I have been underscoring the difficulties of measuring the separate contributions of the several sources of greater efficiency. If no one is yet able to supply anything better than guesses on their magnitude, where do we stand, what do we know?

This much, at least, we have learned: first, the sources of growth in efficiency, and therefore also in labor productivity, are many in number and various in kind; but second, our understanding of them is still very limited. This is an important lesson. It has serious implications for the policies we should pick to raise or maintain the rate of growth of labor productivity and for the degree to which we must regard these policies as experimental and thus be ready to shift their direction and emphasis, even retreat on occasion, as we learn from experience.

PART III

Productivity and
Other Economic Changes

==

CHAPTER VII

Productivity and Business Cycles

Long-term trends in productivity have transformed the world in which we live and work and will continue to do so in the decades and centuries ahead. That is why we have been concentrating our attention on them. But the short-term fluctuations twined around the trends, which we noticed in Chapter II, are also significant. Responsible men in and out of government watch these short-term movements, along with other economic facts, as they chart the business conditions with which they must reckon.

It is therefore worth asking whether anything like a regular pattern can be found in the short-term behavior of labor productivity. If there is such a systematic cyclical pattern, how is it related to the fluctuations that trouble our economic life, the alternation of slow and rapid growth of national output, of growing and declining unemployment?

The annual data for the United States analyzed in Chapter II have already told us that labor productivity generally rises less rapidly when national output is falling and more rapidly when national output is expanding. Since 1889 there have been seventeen times when output fell from one year to another. During some of these years, output per man-hour actually fell. Indeed, declines in output per man-hour were so numerous or so sharp in the seventeen years of falling output that the average rate of change in output per man-hour during these years was *negative,* —0.6 percent per year. During the other sixty-odd years, when total output and general business rose, the average rate of increase in output per man-hour was 3.4 percent per annum. The annual average change for all years, 2.4 percent, is of course the weighted combination of the 3.4 percent for years of rising output and —0.6 percent for years of falling output.

Because the annual indexes involve a great deal of estimation and the piecing out of scanty data, it is encouraging to find confirmation of the results in other sources of information. These are limited largely to manufacturing industries and cover only the more recent decades, but they are more reliable. They have the advantage also of providing information on a monthly basis, which is far more satisfactory for the study of cyclical fluctuations than are annual data.

Being more sensitive, the monthly data on output per man-hour reveal two striking facts entirely missing from the annual figures. As was shown by the annual data, interruptions in the rise in output per man-hour have come mainly during business contractions, when output was falling. But the monthly data also tell us that most of the interruptions were concentrated in the first half of a business contraction rather than continuing over the whole contraction. During the second half of a contraction, output per man-hour was no longer stagnant or even declining. On the contrary, well before general business and output had begun to revive, output per man-hour had resumed its upward march.

After the turn came and business and output were improving, output per man-hour rose even more rapidly than it had before the revival of business and output. But the increase did not continue at so swift a pace all through the expansion. The monthly data tell us that the rate of increase of output per man-hour also changed during the expansion phase of the business cycle. After expansion had pushed output beyond previous peak levels so that it was then scaling new heights, the rise in output per man-hour usually slowed down. Seldom, however, did the speed of increase in output per man-hour during the latter stages of business expansion become as slow as it did during the first half of business contraction.

The average rates of change in output per man-hour in manufacturing industries during the ten business cycles between 1919 and 1961 tell the story most crisply:

Cycle Phase	AVERAGE ANNUAL RATE OF CHANGE IN OUTPUT PER MAN-HOUR
First half of business contraction	0.8%
Second half of business contraction	2.8%
First half of business expansion	5.3%
Second half of business expansion	3.0%

It is worth noting that these figures are based on a comparison of output with wage earner man-hours alone. Had the comparison been made with hours worked by all employees, including salary earners—for whom appropriate monthly information is still largely lacking—the contrast between expansion and contraction would be even greater. The reason is that employment of salary earners, who number up to about a fourth of all factory employees these days, is less responsive to changes in output than is employment of wage earners. Output per hour worked by wage earners and salaried workers combined, then, would probably rise more rapidly than output per wage earner hour during expansion, would fall more rapidly during the initial stages of contraction, and would rise less rapidly during the later stages of contraction. Shifts would still be found, however, in the rate of increase in labor productivity between the first and second halves of expansion and between the first and second halves of contraction.

In industries in which salaried personnel predominate—trade and services, for example—output per man-hour would more frequently tend to decline during the contraction phases than it would in industries manned largely by wage earners. It is because trade and the service industries are such a significant part of the economy that national output per man-hour has often fallen during business contractions.

What we have been tracing is, of course, an average pattern. Output per man-hour did not conform closely to this pattern in every business cycle. With few exceptions, however, behavior in each cycle does bear a recognizable family resemblance to the average.

The most recent business expansion, which began in 1961, provides an illustration. (Because it is the longest peacetime expansion on record, the story for this expansion is told well enough by the annual data.) Output per man-hour in the total private economy rose most rapidly (4.7 percent per annum) between 1961 and 1962, less rapidly (3.7 percent per annum) between 1962 and 1964, and least rapidly (2.8 percent per annum) between 1964 and 1966. Economists who were aware of the pattern of short-term fluctuation in labor productivity were not surprised by the slowdown in 1964–66. Indeed, they were able to predict it.

The "overhead" or "fixed-cost" character of a substantial fraction of the labor employed in manufacturing and other industries—noted in the comment on salaried workers—points to one of the factors that account for the way labor productivity changes during business expansion and contraction. A larger volume of output can be produced not only with more people and longer hours but also—up to a point—with more intensive or effective work on the part of the "regular hands." Output per man-hour tends to rise. Then, during the slack season, as customers become scarce, there is some relaxation of effort and effectiveness, and output per man-hour tends to fall.

But there is much more than this to the explanation of cycles in labor productivity. The changing cyclical pattern is the net result of many diverse factors pushing in different directions. Some tend to speed up labor productivity. Some tend to slow it down. Further, these factors change in relative importance during the cycle.

During the initial stages of expansion, when output is rising rapidly but is still below the level at which most establishments are designed to operate with maximum technical efficiency, increases in the percentage of capacity utilized contributes substantially to increasing labor productivity. The fact already mentioned—the spreading of "overhead" labor over a larger volume of production—is one way in which this occurs. Another is the shift from short hours per worker toward a more normal level. This reduces the waste that subnormal hours per day or days per week entail. Further, new and technologically more advanced plant capacity, ordered during the preceding period of prosperity, is now available to handle additional production requirements. Also, although workers are being added to the payroll, unemployment is still high, and it is not yet necessary for employers to be content with hiring a disproportionately large number of untrained workers.

As expansion proceeds, however, the percentage of capacity utilized may reach its most efficient level. Further increases in capacity utilization contribute little or nothing to the further expansion of labor productivity. Also, here and there obsolescent equipment may have to be brought back into use to meet the pressure of orders. Hours of labor, which have been rising, come to exceed the normal length of the workday, and the overtime strains both workers and equipment. With unemployment now down to low levels, labor shortages make necessary the recruitment of less desirable candidates in order to fill open jobs. Furthermore, the maintenance of discipline becomes more difficult when overtime prevails, jobs are plentiful, and management is overworked. Shortages occur not only in the labor market but also in other markets and in transport facilities. Delays in the deliveries of materials, parts, and supplies grow longer and more frequent. In short, labor productivity continues to rise, but less rapidly than before.

Eventually the business expansion reaches its end, and a recession begins. This means declining output and also, sooner or later, less than optimum use of plant and labor. If this were the only factor, it would push labor productivity down. But accompanying the decline in output are also reversals in the conditions that tended to depress labor productivity during the preceding expansion. These developments now tend to raise labor productivity. The net effect varies from industry to industry and cycle to cycle because industries and cycles differ in the relative importance of the plus and minus factors involved. (I have already mentioned that salaried [that is, overhead] labor is more important in trade and service than in manufacturing.) Sometimes the net effect seems to be little net change in productivity, sometimes a decline. In either case, output per man-hour generally rises less rapidly than during the preceding business expansion.

As the contraction continues, new and technologically superior capacity is finally installed. The high point in installation of new equipment comes, in fact, some time after the beginning of contraction. The slackening of business makes time and energy available for "shaking down" the new equipment and "combing out its bugs." The available work is shifted from old to new equipment, which usually saves labor. In addition, the conditions during prosperity that made for a poorer quality of labor and management are replaced by conditions that make for a better quality. Although output is still falling, it is doing so less rapidly, as a rule, and efforts to adjust to low levels of utilization of capacity are finally showing results. The forces making for higher labor productivity grow stronger, and labor productivity resumes its upward movement.

Once output turns the corner, labor productivity spurts ahead, and the cycle is repeated.

The various factors that help to explain the cyclical behavior of labor productivity can be classified in the same way as we have classified the factors that account for the long-term trend in labor productivity. That is, we can distinguish cyclical fluctuations in three sets of factors—in the quality of labor, in the volume of tangible capital employed per man-hour, and in the efficiency with which labor and capital are used.

Superimposed on the rising long-term trend in the quality of labor is a cyclical fluctuation that reflects, among other things, shifts in the proportions of trained and untrained workers and in the effort exerted by workers as changes occur in hours of labor and in the risk of unemployment. Superimposed on the rising long-term trend in the quantity of tangible capital used per man-hour is a cyclical fluctuation that reflects changes in the rate of investment and in the use of obsolescent equipment. Superimposed on the rising long-term trend in the efficiency with which labor and capital are used is a cyclical fluctuation that reflects such factors as the changing frequency with which stoppages occur because of short production runs or delays occur because of bottlenecks in suppliers' and transporters' facilities.

No specific measurements of the three cycles have as yet been made, but there is good reason to suppose that the three cycles differ somewhat in timing and probably also in amplitude.

The cycle we observe in labor productivity is, we might say, a "weighted average" of the three cycles. Because these weights shift from one cycle to another dur-

ing the course of economic development, it is not surprising that productivity cycles differ somewhat from
one period to another.

The cyclical pattern of labor productivity has interesting implications for the causes of business cycles.

During the later stages of business expansion, labor
shortages are pushing up wage rates more rapidly than
at earlier stages. Yet it is just at this time that the rate
of increase in labor productivity begins to slacken. As a
result of this combination of more rapidly rising wages
and less rapidly rising labor productivity, labor costs per
unit of product begin to rise more rapidly than before.
This acceleration in what, in most industries, is a major
element of costs tends, in turn, to depress profit per
unit of output. In addition, during the later stages of
expansion, output, although still rising, is usually rising
less rapidly than in the middle and early stages. When
retardation of growth in output is strong, the decline in
profit per unit may be sufficient to push even aggregate
profits down before the peak in volume of business is
reached.

These developments in costs, profits per unit, and
aggregate profits have obvious effects on the expectations of businessmen and investors generally. They contribute to the decline in investment commitments that
generally helps to bring on a recession.

Once a contraction is under way, labor productivity
rises even less rapidly or even declines, as we have seen.
However, wage rates may continue to move up, at least
for a while. Unit labor costs may therefore rise no less
rapidly and sometimes even more rapidly during the
first stages of contraction than during the latter stages

of expansion. This continued rise in labor costs, when output is falling and selling prices are weak, serves to intensify the forces making for contraction.

As the contraction proceeds, however, a change occurs. During the latter stages of contraction, labor productivity turns up. And with mounting unemployment the rise in wage rates slows down. As a result, unit labor costs stop rising and then decline, with cheerful consequences for profit prospects. Profit margins may actually begin to rise and with them the investment commitments that help to bring the contraction to a close.

Many factors are involved in the intricate process that generates the cyclical path along which our economy grows. Productivity is only one of the factors. But it is one that plays an intimate role, both as cause and as consequence, as we see, not only in the growth but also in the fluctuations of our economy.

In our discussion of productivity during business cycles we have touched on the short-term relation between wages and productivity. But there is a long-term relation between them as well, which now deserves our attention.

CHAPTER VIII

Productivity and the Rise
of Wages and Salaries

Three quarters of a century ago the average worker in the United States earned something like fifteen to twenty cents an hour in wage or salary. His "fringe benefits," when there were any, were negligible. Today his hourly earnings are more like three dollars. Inclusion of fringe benefits would push the figure up by another 10 percent.

What caused this multiplication of average earnings by a factor of twenty?

Two main causes determine the national average of hourly earnings. One is the general price level, and the other is national productivity. We shall put the general price level aside for the moment and come back to it at a later point. Let us deflate wage and salary increases by the consumer price index, which has more than tripled since 1889. Deflating out the rise in the general price level leaves a sixfold increase in *real* average wages and salaries per hour (including fringe benefits). Now let us concentrate our attention on the relation between this rise in real wages and salaries and the corresponding rise in productivity.

When I say that productivity is the major determinant of the trend in real wages and salaries, you may ask—if you have read the earlier chapters—"Which productivity?" Is it total productivity, our measure of efficiency in the use of labor and capital? Or is it labor productivity—output per man-hour? Or is it, maybe, something in between?

These questions are not academic. When the index of total productivity was first constructed, only a few years ago, some members of the business community welcomed it because they thought that it was a more appropriate index for use in wage negotiations than output per man-hour, and it had the advantage from their point of view of having risen less rapidly than labor productivity. The labor union people disliked the new total productivity index for equally obvious reasons.

There are two ways to determine which productivity is the major determinant of the nation's average real wage and salary. One is to consider the basic forces that operate in the labor market and decide which productivity index best summarizes the influence of these forces. The other is to appeal to history and see which productivity index has most closely matched the index of national real wages and salaries in the past. Of course, the two ways are not independent. What economists know about the labor market rests heavily on their analysis of history. But it is convenient to make the distinction and take up each separately.

A person reading the daily newspaper or walking by a picket line would suppose that the major market forces

see Fuchs
Sector
diff b-
right

affecting real wages are labor unions, which try to raise wages; businessmen who try to keep wages down; and government, which sometimes seems to be trying to do both. Of course, all market forces operate through men —workers, employers, government officials. But it is wrong to think of these men as influencing earnings only when they engage in the kind of large-scale negotiations that get into the newspapers.

In the long run, workers influence the real wages and salaries they receive mainly by devoting time and effort and money to improving the quality of the labor services they can offer and by moving from jobs that pay less to jobs that pay more. Unions are important in labor-management relations, it is true. They influence the conditions of work, and undoubtedly, also, the money wages (and even the real wages) received by their own membership. There may also be some "spillover" effects on the wages of nonunion workers in the unionized industries. But unions have only a modest (if any) effect on the *general* level of real wages. In part, this is because less than a fourth of the labor force is unionized. In part, also, it is because the power of a union—even the strongest—is limited by competition between its members and workers in other industries or other places (sometimes other countries) and by competition between its members and machines or other labor substitutes. When the wages in industry are pushed up too rapidly, the work tends to be shifted to workers elsewhere or to substitutes that would otherwise be too expensive.

In the long run, businessmen influence the wages and salaries they pay by activities aimed at making profits for themselves. They develop new products, try new materials, improve methods of production, open new markets, invest in more and better capital equipment. They seek the labor needed to work their equipment and to use the new methods and materials. They may often go to considerable expense to teach their help to work with the new machinery, methods, and materials by training the workers on the job. And they combine their labor, capital and technology in the most efficient manner they can to produce the old and new products that offer the best prospects of profits.

Businessmen in an industry may get together to fight a large wage increase; but it is just as true that they are almost always competing for labor with one another, with other industries, and sometimes with other countries. When Henry Ford, half a century ago, sought to attract southern workers with what was then the phenomenal wage of five dollars a day or when, more recently, Cluett Peabody moved some of its shirt factories to mining areas to secure help, they were raising wages.

In the long run, government influences the real wages and salaries received by workers throughout the country less by intervening in the wage-determination process than by other activities. Real wages are pulled up when government devotes its energies to strengthening law and order, improving public services, removing physical and other obstacles to trade and the movement of people, capital, and enterprise, educating the young and informing the old, stabilizing the economy, and supporting the research and other activities that can yield rich returns to society at large. Minimum wage laws, for example, like school attendance laws, generally follow rather than lead the prevailing practice in the United States.

In short, the average national real wage and salary rate is pushed up mainly by improvement in the quality of labor, by investment in tangible capital, and by increased efficiency in the use of labor and capital. An increase in any of these three main factors will exert an upward pressure on average wages and salaries by making labor more valuable in production. For, in the long run at least, there is enough competition to ensure labor a wage or salary commensurate with its value in production.

Of the several productivity indexes that can be constructed, it is the index of national labor productivity—output per man-hour—that reflects all three of the influences named, appropriately combined. Output per unit of labor and capital, as we have seen, measures only one of these factors, the increase of efficiency.

We may expect, therefore, that the trend in the national real earnings rate will move most closely with the trend in the national labor productivity index. Does history support this expectation?

The historical facts are clear. There is a close similarity between rates of change in real earnings and in labor productivity when the rates are measured by trends over the entire three quarters of a century between 1889 and 1965. However, there is a lesser degree of similarity when shorter-term trends are compared. And when year-to-year changes are compared, there is little similarity.

Recall the figures cited at the opening of the chapter. The real average hourly earnings of wage and salary workers of the United States rose by 500 percent between 1889 and 1965. In terms of an average rate, these wages and salaries rose by something like 2.5 percent. This figure is surprisingly close to the 2.4 percent average annual rate of increase in output per man-hour.

Because both estimates—earnings as well as productivity —are subject to fairly wide margins of error, the high degree of similarity may be something of a coincidence. Yet it is safe to say, for the estimates are not so poor, that, for the period 1889–1965 as a whole, real earnings and labor productivity moved up closely together— more closely, it should be noted, than did real earnings and total productivity. The rate of increase of real hourly earnings, about 2.5 percent, was much higher than the 1.7 percent rate for output per unit of labor and capital. The historical facts confirm the answer we have given to the question, "Which productivity?"

The similarity between trends in real hourly earnings and trends in labor productivity is less marked when the period between 1889 and 1965 is broken in the 1920's into two subperiods and trends within each of the subperiods are compared. Between 1889 and the 1920's, real hourly earnings rose at an average annual rate of about 1.7 percent and labor productivity at an average annual rate of 2 percent. Between the 1920's and the present, real hourly earnings rose at an average annual rate of 3 percent, and labor productivity at an average annual rate of 2.6 percent. The differences between the rates of change in earnings and labor productivity seem more pronounced than the similarities.

There is an interesting similarity, however, between the *changes* in the two trends. In *both* real hourly earnings and labor productivity, trends in the more recent period were more sharply upward than trends in the earlier period.

When we shift our focus to the year-to-year changes, the relation between real hourly earnings and output per man-hour becomes far more attenuated. Annual changes in labor productivity were uneven, as we saw in Chapter II. So also were annual changes in real hourly earnings. But the year-to-year changes in the rate of growth of labor productivity were not matched in any simple way, if at all, by corresponding movements in real hourly earnings. The two fluctuated more or less independently.

We may conclude that the historical facts are consistent with the reasoning of generations of economists: that of all the factors that determine the long-term trend in the general level of real wages, the three covered by the index of output per man-hour are of outstanding importance in an economy free enough to let the factors work out their effects. But in determining the short-term movements of earnings, factors other than labor productivity play a larger role.

Let us be clear on what this means. The three factors mentioned—greater efficiency, larger volume of tangible capital per man-hour and better labor quality—are indeed the major factors underlying the rise in real hourly earnings. However, they do not exert their effects without delay, interference, or interruption. Sometimes changes in real earnings from one year to the next are substantially greater than the corresponding changes in output per man-hour, and sometimes they are substantially less. Sometimes, in fact, the two move in opposite directions. This is so because other factors, which wash out in the long run, also play their part and are important in the short run.

To illustrate: Changes in the general level of prices were put aside, the reader will recall, when we decided to concentrate on *real* earnings and for that reason deflated money earnings by the consumer price index. This procedure is sufficient to exclude the effects of changes in price levels from the long-term trend of real earnings.

But it cannot exclude all the effects of price level changes from the shorter-term changes in real earnings. Delays are frequent in the response of money wages to changes in the cost of living; and delays may be even longer in the response of salary rates to changes in the cost of living. A speeding-up of price inflation, for example, will tend to be followed by a speeding up of the rate of increase in wages and salaries, but for a time there may be a *decline* in the rate of growth of *real* wages and salaries. Indeed, when the price level accelerates very sharply, real salaries and even real wage rates may actually fall for a while, not simply rise less rapidly than before.

This illustrates why a full explanation of the historical changes in the level of real wages and salaries—which we are not going to tackle here—would have to take account not only of the trend in output per man-hour but also of the behavior of money wages, retail prices, and productivity during the business cycles and the longer periods of price inflation and deflation that are found in the record of the past three quarters of the century. And it would have to take account of still other factors peculiar to particular periods as well as of the more or less gradual changes in the structure and competitiveness of the markets for labor, goods, and capital that have taken place over the years. Yet it is fair to say that the *chief* determinants of the *trends* in the national level of real wages are those measured by national output per man-hour.

Now, all this may well be true of the trend in the *general* level of real wages, but what about the trend of wages in individual industries? Is not the wage in a particular industry greatly affected by the industry's own productivity? And does not the latter, as the reader has been told, sometimes move up much faster or slower than national productivity?

Here, too, an answer can be given on the basis of economic reasoning. Suppose wage and salary rates in the electric power utilities, in tire manufacturing, or in any of the industries in which labor productivity had risen very rapidly were, in fact, pushed up by their rapid increases in labor productivity. Suppose, also, that wage and salary rates in sawing and planning mills, barbering, or other industries in which labor productivity had risen very slowly were held down by their slow increases in labor productivity. What would result? Disparities in wages and salaries between these two groups of industries would become enormous—indeed, quite untenable. Even the most severe obstacles to competition, obstacles not only between workers, but also between workers and substitutes for workers in the form of machines and materials, could not preserve such disparities. In fact, large disparities could not arise in the first place, except in the most exceptional circumstances, or last very long when they did appear.

The historical information on trends in individual industries supports this reasoning. The long-term rise in real hourly earnings in an industry has been closely related to the rise in national output per man-hour but not to the rise in that industry's own output per man-hour. In fact, the relationship between the long-term change in an industry's hourly earnings and the long-term change in its own output per man-hour is negligible. This means that trends in the real wages of individual industries, as well as the trend of the national average real wage, were dominated by the economy-wide factors summarized by the trend in national output per man-hour. Hourly earnings in individual industries moved up more or less together—something to be expected in an economy in which workers and employers respond to wage differentials.

We do not find *closely* parallel changes among the average rates of wages paid by different industries, however, and it would be surprising if we did. The American economy is one in which economic advance has brought not only greater efficiency, improved quality of labor, and more tangible capital per worker but also other changes—in the type of labor used by different industries, in the relative scarcity of the skills they employ, in the values placed on the various nonpecuniary advantages and disadvantages of working in them, and in other determinants of demand and supply. So continuous has the flow of these changes been that adjustment to them has never been completed. Exceptions to the rule that wages in different industries moved together, paralleling national output per man-hour, are therefore also to be expected, and these exceptions appear in the record.

Before we leave the relation between trends in real earnings and trends in productivity, another question must be asked and answered, and a qualification added to what has been said.

If we averaged the long-term rises in real hourly earnings in individual industries and compared this average with the corresponding rise in real hourly earnings in the country as a whole, we would find a difference between the two. The former would be smaller than the latter. In fact, real hourly earnings in most industries rose less rapidly than average hourly earnings in the country as a whole and less rapidly also than national output per man-hour. Why should this be, and what does it mean?

To answer this question, let us start by noting that a rise in the average hourly earnings of all workers in the United States can be split into two components: One is the average of the rises in the wages received in each of the thousands of occupations among which the millions of workers of the United States are distributed, each occupation being defined narrowly enough to apply to a fixed level of skill and educational requirement. The second component is the rise that occurs as more and more young people (and older people also) train themselves for higher skilled jobs or better professional careers, and the number of workers in the occupations requiring higher quality labor (and paying more per hour) increases more rapidly than the number of workers in the occupations using lower quality labor (and paying less per hour).

The average earnings of all workers in the country can rise, even if the second component is zero—that is, even if no increase occurs in the average quality of labor in the United States. For earnings in every occupation rise because of the upward pressures on real wages that result from increases in tangible capital per worker and increases in the efficiency of utilization of labor and capital. Obviously, also, the average earnings of all workers in the country can rise even if the first component is zero—that is, even if tangible capital per worker and efficiency in the use of labor and capital remain constant. For the national average of earnings rises as relatively more youngsters shift away from the less advanced occupations, which pay low wages or salaries, and shift toward the more advanced occupations, which pay high wages or salaries. In fact, of course, both components have been greater than zero. The average earnings of all workers in the country has risen by the sum of (1) the average rise in individual occupations *and* (2) the rise resulting from improved labor quality and the shift to better paying occupations.

This analysis leads to the conclusion that the trend in real wages or salaries of workers in a *given* ("average") occupation has been determined not by the three factors —labor quality, tangible capital, and efficiency—but only by two of these, namely, tangible capital and efficiency. It can be shown that the two factors are summarized by an index of national output per *weighted* man-hour—that is, an index that compares output with a total of man-hours in which an hour of high-grade labor counts for more than an hour of low-grade labor. This index of output per weighted man-power falls between the two indexes to which we have limited our attention up to this point.

Now to answer the question posed earlier: The average of the rises in earnings in individual industries is less than the average for all workers in the country, because the former excludes the rise—or more correctly, a good deal of the rise—associated with improved labor quality. The average of the rises in earnings in individual industries moves more closely with national output per weighted man-hour, because national output per weighted man-hour excludes the effect on labor productivity of the rise in labor quality—or, more correctly, excludes the effect of a good deal of the rise in labor quality.

I add the qualification because in most of the available statistical compilations individual industries are defined too broadly and therefore include too many kinds and qualities of labor (which are always changing in relative importance) for their earnings to be entirely free of the effects of change in quality. We will have to come back to this qualification when we discuss policies to "guide" future changes in wages by means of productivity indexes.

CHAPTER IX

Productivity and Price Trends

Not many people are still around who remember what Henry Ford's revolutionary methods did to the price of automobiles. By concentrating on a single car, the Model T, Ford departed from the costly, almost "custom-made," manufacturing process of the early 1900's. "Any color, so long as it is black" became his motto. His mass-production methods enabled him to reduce the price of a car from the prevailing several thousand dollars to something like $800 or $900. Then, by installing the moving assembly line into his factory, Ford cut costs still further. By the time World War I broke out, the price of the Model T was down to $500. Further improvements in production methods, and more economies of mass production, enabled Ford to cut the price even more. Despite the wartime rise in the general price level, the Model T was well under $400 in the early 1920's.

More recent is the experience with the prices of such

products as refrigerators, radios, nylons, plastics, and antibiotics. Many people know what happened to these prices as the industries turning out the products learned to be more and more efficient and raised their productivity sharply. But let me recall one bit of this industrial history. The wholesale price of streptomycin, in bulk per thousand grams, was as much as $16,000 early in 1946. It was $2,800 a year later, $1,300 two years later, and after ten years, it was down to $75. It is around $30 today.

This is not the whole story, of course. Many people have also had personal experience with industries, such as lumber, in which productivity has been slow to rise over the years and prices have moved up much more rapidly than the general price level.

Indeed, anyone who has kept his eyes open realizes that the productivity of an industry and the prices customers have to pay for its products are somehow related. This relationship is important. When an industry's prices decline relative to other prices, more people buy its products; and customers already buying it buy more. The benefits derived from the industry's progress are distributed widely.

Further, when an industry's products become relatively cheaper and its sales expand, additional opportunities for employment, and for investment as well, may be opened up. Rapid increases in an industry's productivity, when reflected in lower prices and higher output, can mean hirings, not firings, as we shall see in Chapter X.

Examples are informative, but we want to know more about the relationship between the productivity and the prices of industries than examples alone can tell us. That is, we want to know just what the relationship is, and how strong it is. For this purpose it is necessary to determine the changes over a period of years in the productivity and in the prices of a large variety of industries and then to compare the changes with one another.

To avoid possible confusion, let us keep in mind that we will *not* examine the relationship between change in the general level of prices and change in *overall* productivity. The strategic variable determining the general price level is the supply of money. It is not the only factor, since the price level depends also on the supply of goods and services that is being "chased" by the money and on the amount of cash people want to hold. Productivity does help determine the supply of goods and services. This effect was especially important in determining the declining trend in prices in the United States following the Civil War. But productivity is usually only a minor element in the determination of the general price level.

What we *are* concerned with are changes in the productivity and prices of *individual* industries. We ask this particular question: Are the industries in which productivity has increased most rapidly also the industries in which selling prices have increased least rapidly, or even fallen? And we ask, at the same time: Have slow increases in productivity—hardly any industry has experienced a declining productivity trend—been associated with rapid increases in prices? We want, in other words, to know whether the examples cited earlier are exceptional or not.

When we speak of rising or falling prices, therefore, we speak of the prices of an industry rising or falling in relation to the general price level. When, in this context, we speak of a rapid or slow increase in productivity, we mean that the productivity of an industry is rising more or less rapidly than overall, or national, productivity.

Productivity, as we saw in Chapter I, stands not for one concept, but for a family of concepts dealing with the ratio of output to input. Of the two main indexes described in Chapter I, the preferable one for our present purpose is output per unit of labor and capital. This index measures the efficiency with which both capital and labor have been used, and efficiency is a major factor determining total cost per unit, which in turn is important in determining the selling prices of an industry's output. The other index, output per man-hour, is more narrowly focused on an element of labor cost. Labor cost, however, is not as important in determining selling price as are labor and capital costs combined. As we shall see, there is a difference in just how the two productivity indexes are related to price.

What do we find when we make these comparisons between productivity and price for as many industries and for as long a period as possible?

Output per unit of labor and capital, we see, has clearly been inversely related to prices. Our examples, then, were right in suggesting a *general* phenomenon. The industries in which productivity rose most rapidly during the first fifty years of the twentieth century, reported in Chapter III, were usually those in which prices fell over the same period, either absolutely or in relation to the general level of prices. Industries in which productivity lagged were usually those in which prices rose in relation to the general level of prices. At the top of the list, arranged in order of increase in output per unit of labor and capital, are electric light and power, manufactured gas, and rubber products, all industries in which selling prices declined not only relatively but even absolutely. At the other end, among the industries in which productivity lagged, are lumber products—already mentioned—and coal mining, industries in which prices have, since the opening of the century, risen far more than did the general level of prices. Because changes in output per man-hour and changes in output per unit of labor and capital have been closely related, as we saw in Chapter III, much the same picture is found in the relation between relative change in output per man-hour and relative change in price.

With this inverse relationship established, we can ask *how much* of a change in relative price was usually associated with a given change in relative productivity? The same statistics provide the answer. On the average, relative changes in prices have been roughly proportionate to relative changes in output per unit of labor and capital, but in opposite directions. In more exact language, when the relative productivity of an industry was *multiplied* by a given quantity, its relative price tended to be *divided* by the same quantity.

In this respect, however, the relationship between prices and output per man-hour—the particular productivity-price relationship most frequently discussed—differs from the relationship between prices and output per unit of labor and capital. Relative changes in output per man-hour were generally associated with somewhat *smaller* relative changes in prices. Specifically, in industries in which relative output per man-hour doubled, relative prices tended to fall by a third rather than a half.

The correlation between price and output per unit of labor and capital (or output per man-hour) has been far from perfect, however. There were many departures from inverse proportionality. This is why words such as "tended" and "as a rule," or "usually" and "roughly," have to be used to describe the relationship between productivity and prices. Indeed, factors other than productivity have been no less important, taken as a group, than productivity in accounting for relative price changes.

We have already suggested why changes in the relative productivity levels of industries would be associated with changes (in the opposite direction) in relative price levels, but it is worth our while to spell out the reasons.

Given time for the necessary adjustments, competition makes for equality of price and cost per unit (including a normal profit), therefore of relative price and relative cost per unit, and therefore also of changes in these. A major determinant of cost per unit is efficiency—output per unit of labor and capital. When efficiency rises, less labor and capital are needed to produce a unit of output, and costs tend to fall. We saw in Chapters III and VI that all, or virtually all, industries have experienced a rise in efficiency. But the rise was large in some industries and small in others. In those industries in which the rise in efficiency was large, costs per unit tended to fall more than in the industries in which the rise in efficiency was modest. Under the pressure of competition, relative prices adjusted themselves accordingly.

The working of competition to bring prices in line with costs, and thus with productivity, does not always appear beneficent to those immediately affected. I once heard the head of a large chemical company complain that because his industry has been enjoying excellent profit margins, companies from other industries had begun to "assail" the industry with "new competition from many quarters." Yet the same businessman, in the same statement, proudly related how his better products were making inroads on the sales of other industries. Both facts illustrate how the free market distributes the gains from increased productivity to society at large.

Although we should expect changes in productivity and price to be related, we should not expect, and we do not find, the relationship to be anything like perfect. Efficiency is a major determinant of price, but it is not the only determinant. The relative price of an industry may therefore change more or less than appears to be warranted by its relative productivity change, even in a fully competitive industry and even given time for adjustment. How much more or less will depend on the importance and behavior of the determinants other than productivity. Sometimes they are so powerful as to cause relative price and productivity to move in the same rather than in opposite directions.

Among these factors—factors that influence the relative prices of an industry's products but are not covered by our measure of efficiency—are changes in the efficiency with which materials, fuel, and services purchased from other industries are put to use. When fuel, for example, is especially important to an industry, as it is to electric power stations, and economies in the utilization of fuel have been very great, the costs and therefore the relative prices of the industry will tend to fall more than would be suggested by the change in its efficiency in the use of labor and capital alone. The result will be the same if an industry has learned to get much more out of its raw materials by using better extractive processes and by turning wastes into useful by-products, as has the cottonseed products industry, or if it has learned to make a more satisfactory product with a thinner coating of protective material, as has the tinplate industry.

The relation between price and output per unit of labor and capital will be altered also in industries that have increased their purchases of materials, fuel, and the like, per unit of product, in order to economize on their own labor and tangible capital. The outstanding example of our generation is farming, in which the production of motive power—raising horses, mules, and oxen, and the feed to keep them going—has largely been turned over to the industries producing tractors, gasoline, and electricity. If there were enough quantitative information, we could compute a productivity index that took account of changes in the use of materials and supplies per unit of product. We would get such an index by comparing output with total input, including not only labor and capital in input but also materials and supplies. This index, mentioned in Chapter III, would be preferable to other productivity indexes for analyzing price change. But the necessary information is largely lacking.

The prices that an industry has to pay for its inputs are also involved. When these prices rise more rapidly than the prices paid by other industries—all other changes being equal—we may expect the relative selling prices of the industry to rise more rapidly than would be indicated solely by the change in the industry's own relative productivity.

The prices of different raw materials, fuel, and equipment do not move closely together, for the industries producing them do not experience similar rates of productivity increase. Even wage rates (which move much more closely together in different industries than do other input prices, for reasons given in the preceding chapter) do not exactly parallel one another. In effect, then, the factory price of a refrigerator will reflect changes in the efficiency of *every* industry that is directly or indirectly involved in the production of refrigerators —not only refrigerator manufacturing, but also trucking, power, and the industries that produce electric motors and compressors, cartons, steel sheet, paints, and so on. Looking in the other direction, the productivity of the paint manufacturing industry, and the price of paint, will influence the price of all products in which paint is used—which means virtually every product. But the influence of the price of paint will be greater in some cases than in others. The relation between any particular industry's relative price and relative productivity is thus bound to be loose.

When an industry is not fully competitive, that, too, may influence the relation between the price of the products and its productivity. The adjustment of prices to changes in productivity will be impeded. But this is largely a short-run factor, usually overcome in time. In the long run, competition tends to prevail in most industries.

When the period of time is short, however, imperfections of competition and other factors make for more and bigger differences between changes in relative price and in relative productivity than when the period is long. Lags become important. Less time is available for adjustments of prices to costs as conditions alter. Even with allowance for anticipations, the correlation between price and productivity is weaker.

The immediate impact of increased demand, for example, is largely on price and profits. Prices go up and so do profits. Until new plants are constructed by companies already in the industry, or by outsiders attracted by the high profits, prices will be "out of line" with costs and with productivity. Decreases in demand work in the other direction. The initial impact is on relative prices and profits, and prices will remain out of line with costs and productivity until capacity has been retired.

There are also temporary rises and falls in demand during business expansions and contractions of the kind described in Chapter VII. These cyclical changes in demand, and the other developments that take place during business cycles, will make the short-term relation between prices and productivity somewhat different from the long-term relation. The difference will be greater in the "cyclically sensitive" industries than in those with stabler demand.

All this raises some questions on the proposition that change in the prices of an industry should be judged, or even controlled, by change in its productivity. We will examine this idea and the proposal frequently made for a productivity guideline for wages in Chapter XI.

CHAPTER X

Productivity and Shifts in Employment

Along with the editor of *The New Yorker*, a lot of people have been uneasily eyeing a subway advertisement that pictures a complicated-looking electrical unit and inquires, "When this circuit learns your job, what are you going to do?"

There is no doubt that automation, mechanization, or any advance that makes for higher labor productivity can wipe out jobs. The hand-loom weavers, the cigarmakers, the cotton pickers—history is thronged with workers who could bear witness to the suffering caused by labor-saving developments. But theirs is not the entire story, nor even the larger part of it. The fact is that the question, "When this circuit learns your job, what are you going to do?" is one of those "Have you stopped beating your wife?" questions that no one should answer quickly or can ever answer simply.

It is true that the direct effect of increases in productivity—which for this purpose is best measured by output per man-hour—is to reduce employment. Increase in an industry's output per man-hour is identical with a reduction in the number of man-hours the industry employs *per unit of output*. All other things being equal, this reduction in employment per unit makes for a reduction in the industry's aggregate employment. The bigger the rate of increase in the industry's output per man-hour—ignoring its indirect effects—the bigger is the direct pressure on the employment it offers.

But there *are* indirect effects of productivity increases, and these may not be ignored. All other things, in other words, are *not* equal. A rise in an industry's productivity presses down also on the price of the industry's product. As we learned in Chapter IX, the more rapidly productivity rises, the greater tends to be the reduction in selling price. If demand is at all responsive to price—and it would be extraordinary if demand were entirely inelastic—output will rise and thus partially restrain the effect of higher output per man-hour. If demand is sufficiently responsive to the decline in price, the resulting rise in output could even exceed the rise in output per man-hour. The number of man-hours worked in the industry would then go up, not down.

The historical record informs us that this event is not at all infrequent. In the long run, industries in which productivity has risen more rapidly than in the economy as a whole have often raised their employment by a *larger* percentage than did industry generally and not by a smaller percentage, as might be supposed. And we find, correspondingly, that industries in which productivity has seriously lagged have often raised their employment *less* than industry generally or have actually cut employment. In Chapter IX, we cited the electric light and power industry as an example of an industry with a rapidly rising trend in productivity and rapidly falling trend in relative price; it is also one with rapidly rising trends in output and employment. The lumber-mill products industry, on the other hand, which has been lagging in productivity and raising its prices, has had a record of lagging output and falling employment.

Examples can be found not only in manufacturing and the public utilities but also in other sectors of the economy. In barber shops, output per man-hour has barely gone up since 1939, while employment of barbers has grown not at all. In the broiler-raising industry, output per man-hour has risen at a phenomenal rate since the 1930's—and so has the number of persons engaged in this branch of farming.

Indeed, the historical record gives more than just examples of an association of relatively high trend rates of increases in productivity with high trend rates of increases in employment, and lagging increases in productivity with lagging employment. The record indicates that over the long run a better than average increase in an industry's productivity *usually*—not merely sometimes, but more often than not—meant a better than average increase in employment and that a less than average increase in productivity was accompanied by a less than average increase (or even a decrease) in employment—again, not merely sometimes, but more often than not.

This fact is not generally known. Yet it is highly significant. It means that increases in output per man-hour can bring opportunities for labor, even in industries in which productivity advances are great. And productivity increases not only can, but have often done so.

The course of employment in an industry reflects not only what has been happening to the industry's own productivity but also what has been happening to productivity in the country at large. This, too, is part of the story.

The increase in national productivity, and the higher income it has brought, has tended to raise the demand for the output of many industries. Higher national productivity has in this way supported or increased the demand for workers in these industries and often offset the direct effects of the industries' own productivity changes when these effects tended to be adverse to employment in these industries.

Especially great, of course, were the effects of increased income on the output and employment of industries that produce the goods and services that people buy more freely as they grow richer. Although these were often industries in which productivity lagged and costs and prices rose, the record shows that increased national productivity helped sustain and often raise employment in them. People wanted the products of these industries even though those products had become more expensive; with their incomes advancing, they were able to pay the higher prices. Many of the health service industries provide examples of rising prices accompanied by rising rather than falling demand.

Nor is this the end of the story. When population and the total labor forces are increasing, as is almost universally the case, industries in which employment is declining *relatively* may nevertheless be industries in which the *absolute* number of jobs is stable or even rising.

Further, even when an industry's employment is declining absolutely, unemployment is not necessarily created as a result. When the pace of decline is slow enough, the reduction is absorbed by the normal decline in the length of the workweek, one of the fruits of rising productivity.

Normal attrition also plays a part. Put in terms of the example with which we started, before "the circuit learns your job," you may have been given your gold watch at the lunch tendered employees reaching retirement age.

Or, probably more important, you may have gone off quite voluntarily, to a new job making those circuits—or anything that people want more of—because the new job pays better than your old job. For although technological change may destroy jobs, it also creates new jobs to which workers are attracted by better pay even before their old jobs have become obsolete. This is how, years ago, the then new automobile industry in Detroit got its workers from the South. In short, technological change means labor saving in the production of old commodities and services, but it leads to the development and spread of new products, which require more labor.

But we should not blink our eyes to the fact that technological and other changes within an industry can create serious problems of adjustment. Not everybody whose job has been learned by a circuit or a machine is ready for retirement, or has moved off to a new job on the West Coast, or is intellectually and physically able to learn a new trade.

The effects of technological change on particular groups of workers can be serious, more serious than we would estimate when we concentrate our attention solely on the total number employed in an industry. The introduction of the cigar-making machine created new jobs in the cigar industry for machine tenders and equipment maintenance men, but these were jobs for women and mechanics, not jobs for the men whose skill was in fingers trained to roll cigars. Even had total employment in the cigar industry been sustained—which was not the case—the problem of adjustment for the craftsmen would have been severe.

Nor are the problems of adjustment always minor even when the old skills are still in demand, if the open jobs are open only in distant communities.

Technological change may demand adjustment not only to new work and working conditions but also to quite different modes of living. When that is the case, as it has been in many farming communities in recent years, the problem of adjustment becomes especially severe. A recent article on the effects of technological change in farm work in the delta states of Alabama, Louisiana, and Mississippi hardly exaggerated the situation when it spoke of "the demise of the sharecropper."

The problem of the sharecropper illustrates the difficulties that have been plaguing workers in coal mining and on the railroads as well as on farms. Employment in these particular industries has, since the war, been declining with unusual rapidity because productivity in these industries was rising with exceptional vigor, but their output either failed to rise or did not rise high enough to sustain employment.

This experience has attracted a good deal of attention. People have been asking whether the problem of adjustment to technological change (and to the other factors that affect employment) has grown more difficult in recent decades. To some, indeed, the "threat of automation" has appeared so serious that they fear that new technologies already in existence will soon eliminate the jobs of most men.

Does the future look so bleak?

Labor productivity has, it is true, been rising more rapidly since the end of the war than has been the country's long-term experience. But the rate of unemployment of the labor force as a whole has not shown an upward trend. Nor, looking to the future, are there signs that the future rate of increase of productivity will be higher than we have recently been experiencing. People talk of revolutionary change because they see economic feasibility in what is only technologically feasible. The two can be very wide apart, however, and the gap between them may require decades or generations to be closed. Immediately after the war, there was much wild speculation about the speed with which atomic energy would displace the conventional sources of electric power. Now, over twenty years later, atomic energy is just barely beginning to be a significant source of power.

Also, the problem of adjustment depends not only on the rate of technological development and the other factors that make labor adjustment necessary but also on the capacity of the country to adjust, and there is evidence that this capacity has grown on net balance. A higher level of education, better transportation and communications, a greater reserve in the form of savings—these, which we have identified among the sources of higher productivity, help also to ease the problem of adjustment.

In addition, improvement has taken place—rapidly in recent years—in aids to adjustment, including unemployment insurance, employment services, retraining programs, and the like. And there has also been improvement in private arrangements, worked out in labor-management agreements, to study and ease the problems of adjustment to technological change. One provision of the contract between General Motors and the United Automobile Workers, concluded late in 1967, provided for the establishment of a joint union-company committee on technological progress "to anticipate and resolve the problems of advancing technology and its impact on U.A.W. members."

These arrangements, public and private, are being established because we are seeking to learn more and do more about the economic problems of our fellow citizens. We are giving a voice to those affected and listening to it; we have raised our sights on the standards we deem proper; and we are widening the responsibilities of government and private business for the well-being of our citizens. Indeed, the problem of adjustment appears more serious today precisely because our standards of well-being are higher. Also, we know much more about unemployment and the distribution of income than we did before the war, when there was nothing like the monthly reports we now have on the state of the economy.

Whether or not the difficulties suffered by workers in adjusting to changes in the labor market are greater now than they were in earlier times, most of us would agree that the suffering should be alleviated.

The solution, it must be stressed, is not to impede technological development or the other factors that make for higher productivity. Higher productivity is the source of the greater economic welfare we want for ourselves and our neighbors. Nor is the solution to cut hours of work so rapidly as to take the fruits of higher productivity in a larger proportion of leisure and a smaller proportion of goods and services than most of us like. Instead, arrangements must be made whereby society as a whole helps shoulder the problems of adjusting to rising productivity—to see to it that these problems do not fall only on the backs of those immediately affected.

What is needed, as the National Commission on Technology, Automation, and Economic Progress recommended in its report early in 1966, is a complex of active public policies. Among these are:

Aggressive fiscal and monetary policies to stimulate growth, for the problem of adjustment to technological change is less difficult when aggregate demand is rising;

Policies to make available adequate educational opportunity to young and old;

Improvements in the supply and distribution of information on jobs and in the means of matching men with jobs;

A permanent program of relocation assistance;

Regional development programs to direct "concerted regional efforts to take advantage of opportunities and avoid dislocation"; and

A program providing, in effect, that "government be an employer of last resort, providing work for the hard-core unemployed in useful community enterprise."

There will be differences of opinion on the urgency, scope, and details of each of the policies included in this list and also on those that are not included. Few, however, will disagree with the commission that "Our society must do a far better job than it has in the past of assuring that the burdens of changes beneficial to society as a whole are not borne disproportionately by some individuals." And when, at the same time, the steps taken also help to improve further the quality of our labor force and the efficiency with which it is used in production—that is, serve to contribute to economic growth rather than impede it—so much the better.

PART IV

Economic Policy and Productivity

CHAPTER XI

Productivity Guideposts for Wages and Prices

Most people who worry about inflation seem to believe in a "profiteer" theory of its causes. Primary responsibility for inflation, they feel, rests in the industries where wages and prices are rising more than they "ought" to. And they believe that these industries can be identified. Once identified, the culprits can be exhorted—or, if need be, compelled—to behave in a socially responsible fashion.

From this point of view, what is needed is a practicable formula that tells how each wage or price ought to behave. With such a formula, presumably we would know when a powerful trade union was asking too big a wage increase or when a company with "excessive market power" was trying to post too high a price.

Formulas that make use of productivity indexes as wage and price "guideposts," as the President's Council of Economic Advisers called them, are the kind that have become familiar here and abroad in recent years.

Every economist would agree that guideposts derived from productivity indexes do make a certain amount of economic sense and have a certain value in judging wage and price changes. We saw in Chapter VIII that output per man-hour in the economy at large summarizes the main forces that determine the trend of real wages in different industries. And in Chapter IX we saw that an industry's productivity trend influences the industry's relative price trend.

Whether the kernel of good economic sense in the guideposts is substantial enough to make them of real practical value is another question, however. Guideposts of the sort set up by the Kennedy Administration in our country and similar formulas developed in Europe have not prevented or even seriously limited price inflation. But is it reasonable to suppose they can really do this job, especially in an economy in which easy money and government deficits are being used to pursue an expansive economic policy and demand is pressing upward on wages and prices? Let us see why guideposts tend eventually to be ignored entirely or, worse, to be followed by compulsory wage and price fixing.

The guideposts that have attracted so much attention in this country in recent years were first set forth by the President's Council of Economic Advisers in 1962. Apart from exceptions—about which more later—these guideposts were not much changed until 1968. Here is how they are described in the various annual reports of the council:

> *The general guidepost for wages* states that "the annual rate of increase of total employee compensation (wages and fringe benefits) per manhour worked"—in any indus-

try—"should equal the national trend rate of increase in output per manhour."

The general guidepost for prices states that "prices should remain stable in those industries where the increase of productivity equals the national trend; that prices can appropriately rise in those industries where the increase of productivity is smaller than the national trend; and that prices should fall in those industries where the increase of productivity exceeds the national trend."

As the council pointed out, "Observance of the guideposts would mean that unit labor costs would decline in the industries where productivity gains are above average, and rise in industries where such gains are below the national average. Average unit labor cost in the economy would remain constant. Similarly, the decrease of prices in industries with above-average increases in productivity would offset the price rises in industries with below-average productivity gains. The average level of prices would remain stable."

If the average level of prices did remain stable, the annual rate of increase of employee compensation per man-hour in ordinary money terms would be identical with the rate of increase of *real* compensation per man-hour. And the price changes referred to in the guidepost for prices would be identical with *relative* price changes.

Now, there is a connection between the national trend rate of increase in output per man-hour and the trend rate of increase in real earnings per man-hour. But the wage guidepost assumes more than this. It refers to the annual rate of increase of real hourly earnings over the *one-, two-, or three-year period of a contract,* not to the *trend* rate of increase in these earnings averaged over a period of many years. These are not the same. Further, the wage guidepost states that the annual rate of increase in earnings should *equal* the trend rate of increase in national output per man-hour, not merely move more or less with it.

Similarly, there is a connection between relative productivity trends and relative price trends. But the price guidepost refers to changes in relative prices *from one year to another,* not to *trends* in prices averaged over a period of years. And it states that these year-to-year changes in relative prices should be exactly proportional to the year-to-year changes in relative productivity, not merely more or less correlated with them. Specifically, according to the guidepost, year-to-year changes in relative prices should be zero in those industries where the increase of productivity equals the national trend of productivity.

Are these sensible rules? Under what conditions— or on what assumptions—will wages and prices behave as the guideposts say they would (or should) in a noninflationary, competitive economy?

Let us begin with the general wage guidepost, noting the conditions under which real hourly earnings and national labor productivity would move together in perfect step—that is, would run *parallel* to one another.

If real hourly earnings and national labor productivity were to move in step, the shares in national income of labor and capital would remain unchanged, and labor and property income would move up together. To see this, recall that real hourly earnings equal real labor income divided by man-hours and that national labor productivity equals total real income (which is essentially the same as national product) divided by man-hours. Then note that from these definitions it follows that identical rates of change in labor income per man-hour and in national product per man-hour must mean identical rates of change in labor income, in total income, and also in property income.

I have heard some people say that there is a "natural" tendency for the proportion of labor to property income to remain constant and that, therefore, it is "right and proper" for real hourly earnings to parallel national labor productivity. But let us be less naïve and ask *why,* or when, this is to be expected.

The labor-income property-income ratio will be stable when percentage *increases* in the quantity of tangible capital's services relative to labor's services are exactly offset by percentage *reductions* in the price of capital's services relative to the price of labor's services. And when will this happen? When these three requirements are met: (1) the percentage increases that take place in the supply of tangible capital relative to the supply of labor lead to equal percentage decreases in the unit value of capital's services relative to the unit value of labor's services; (2) the changes that occur in the efficiency with which labor and capital are used in production are not more or less capital-saving than labor-saving and therefore do not disturb the relative values of the services of labor and capital; and (3) there is sufficient competition to bring the price of labor and of capital into a proportion equal to their relative values in production.

These are rather stringent requirements. Do they hold in fact? The historical evidence suggests that on the whole they do, in so far as *long-term trends* and average hourly earnings in *the economy at large* are concerned. We saw in Chapter VIII that the average real hourly earnings of all workers did rise over the past three quarters of a century at a trend rate about equal to the trend rate of national labor productivity. But this was *not* true of earnings in individual industries— to which, in fact, the guideposts are applied. In that same chapter, we learned that earnings in individual industries tended to move up with national output per *weighted* man-hour, which rose less rapidly than national output per unweighted man-hour.

The first criticism to which we are led, then, is that the wage guidepost is the index of national output per man-hour, rather than the more appropriate index of national output per weighted man-hour (or something between the two productivity indexes). If the wage rate in every industry or occupation were to move up with national output per man-hour and workers benefited not only from these increases but also from increases in earnings resulting from training, upgrading, and shifts from low to high wage industries or occupations —as they do—wages in the economy at large would rise *more* than national output per man-hour. The share of national output received by labor would rise, not remain constant.

As for our second criticism, the trend of national productivity is supposed to serve as a guide to the rate of increase in wages from one year to the next or over the brief two- or three-year period of a wage agreement, not as a guide to the *trend* rate of increase in wages. But there is little ground in history, as our earlier review made clear, for supposing that short-term changes in wages would parallel the trend rate of increase in productivity even in a competitive noninflationary economy. When, for example, business is good, profits are

high, and unemployment is low, the average real wage
—in competitive and noncompetitive industries alike—
usually rises more rapidly than its own trend rate or
than the trend rate of increase in productivity. When
business is poor, profits low, and unemployment widespread, the average real wage usually rises less rapidly
than these trend rates. If wages were to be kept in line
with the trend rate of growth of national labor productivity, wages would move up no more rapidly when
business, employment, and profits were good than when
they were poor and no less rapidly when business, employment, and profits were poor than when they were
good. During periods of good business, then, pressures
on employees to ask and on employers to offer higher
wages than the guideposts indicated would build up in
competitive and noncompetitive industries alike. And
when business was poor, the pressures would be on employers to resist wage increases equal to those indicated
by the guidepost and on workers to accept more modest offers. Compliance with the guidepost on a voluntary (or even involuntary) basis would be severely
limited.

At no time, in fact, are wages and productivity ever
in exact balance. The basic factors that determine the
long-term trend of wages—changes in efficiency, in tangible capital per worker, and in the quality of labor—
require time to work out their effects and make their
impact on wages. This is true even in a competitive
economy and even with allowance for the influence of
expectations on the lags. Year-to-year changes in wages,
therefore, inevitably include upward or downward adjustments made in response to earlier as well as to
current changes in the basic forces summarized in the
national productivity index. And because these adjust-

ments may be greater in some industries than in others, and greater in some years than in other years, no uniform or simple rule can provide for them.

A third source of criticism and controversy is the definition of the "trend" rate of increase in output per man-hour. The problem is largely that of deciding how long or how recent the period should be that we use in calculating the trend rate. But also involved are imperfections in the statistics, with resulting later revisions. As we learned in Chapter II, the average annual rate of increase in output per man-hour over 1956–61 —the original basis used by the council to determine the trend rate—was 3.2 percent. Over 1960–65, with the period different *and* the data revised, the average rate turned out to be 3.6 percent. In addition, when wages are being set for one to three years in the future, the correct criterion is the *expected* trend rate. A question then arises whether past trends in national labor productivity have been characterized by acceleration, long swings, etc. (about which there can be differences of opinion), and whether past trends will continue into the future.

Another, and serious, trouble with the wage guidepost is the assumption that the *major* sources of excessive upward pressure on wages are strong labor unions. This can hardly be true when the consumer price index is rising by 2 or more percent per annum, as it has been during recent years. A group of workers whose wage increase had been kept "in line" with the productivity guidepost over this period would have received not a 3.2 percent per annum increase in *real* wages, but little or no increase. As the council found it necessary to say in its 1968 annual report, "In the face of the 3 percent increase of consumer prices that occurred during 1967, it would be patently unrealistic to expect labor to accept increases in money wages which would represent essentially no improvement in real hourly income." And all that the Council felt it could ask of the labor unions in 1968 was a wage settlement equal not to 3.2 percent but merely "appreciably lower then the 5½ percent average of 1967."

There are other troublesome points that arise when it is asked whether productivity can provide an adequate guidepost for wages. It should be evident by now, however, that the assumptions involved in applying national output per man-hour in wage negotiation and determination are many and that they do not hold fully in every period and in every situation. Some of the deficiencies of the wage guidepost do tend to offset one another, it is true. The use of national output per man-hour, rather than output per weighted man-hour, as the guidepost, would tend to bias real wages upward; the neglect of increases in consumer prices (until they have become too big to be ignored) would tend to bias real wages downward. But there is little reason to expect that these and other deficiencies will balance out completely.

To overcome some of the difficulties posed by the limitations of a general guidepost, recourse may be had to a rule providing for modifications or exceptions. The council constructed such a rule in 1962. As repeated in 1966:

Wage increases above the general guideposts may be desirable

—where wage rates are inadequate for an industry to attract its share of the labor force necessary to meet the demands for its products;

—where wages are particularly low—that is, near the bottom of the economy's wage scales; or

—where changes in work rules create large gains in productivity and substantial human costs requiring special adjustment of compensation.

The rule does not make clear, however, when an exception is justified, or—perhaps more to the point—when an exception is *not* justified. Since frequent exceptions are difficult to administer and will in the end vitiate the rule, there has been a natural tendency on the part of the council to play down exceptions. By 1966, it was asserting that "because the industries in which unions possess strong market power are largely high-wage industries in which job opportunities are relatively very attractive, the first two of these exceptions is rarely applicable." Nor is it surprising that the 1966 formulation of the rule had nothing to say about industries in which wage rate increases might properly fall *short* of the general guide rate. This possibility was recognized in the original 1962 formulation:

Wage rate increases would fall short of the general guide rate in an industry which could not provide jobs for its entire labor force even in times of generally full employment; or in which wage-rates are exceptionally high compared with the range of wages earned elsewhere by similar labor, because the bargaining position of workers has been especially strong.

The two shifts between 1962 and 1966—one playing down grounds for increases above the general guide rate and the other omitting references to grounds for increases below the general guide rate—had to go hand in hand. If many exceptions were permitted for wage increases in excess of those allowed by the general guidepost and few cases—or none—could be expected of wages increasing less than allowed by the general guidepost, the average wage rate would rise significantly more than national output per man-hour.

Another reason for minimizing the possibility of exceptions is the serious difficulty of determining what degree of deviation from the general guidepost is permissible. About this, the rule has nothing to say.

Another basis for exceptions is often mentioned when difficulties encountered in obtaining voluntary adherence to the general guidepost become serious, especially in industries in which productivity and profits have been rising rapidly.

It is then suggested that when labor productivity in an industry is rising more rapidly than national labor productivity, wages in the industry might reasonably rise a bit more rapidly than national productivity. The reverse is presumed for an industry in which productivity is rising less rapidly than national productivity. The guidepost for an industry would then be an average of the national productivity trend and the industry's own productivity trend, with the former being given the larger weight.

A guidepost of this kind was used in the Netherlands —but only for a while. It soon became clear that in many industries an adequate statistical basis for a productivity index was lacking. As a result, wages were frequently negotiated without serious attention being paid to the guidepost. Only after agreement on the wage increase had been reached by management and labor, would they agree on an industry productivity index that made the negotiated wage increase fit the guidepost.

This kind of guidepost will break down sooner or

later for another and more basic reason. Wages in different industries must remain in reasonable relation to one another, whatever the degree of divergence among industries' productivity trends. Even though an industry's productivity trend is given only a small weight in calculating the guidepost, the cumulative effect on the nation's wage structure of adherence to this guidepost must eventually become intolerable.

Most of the criticisms made in discussing the wage guideposts apply also to the price guideposts. Only a few points require emphasis.

One relates to the general price guidepost itself. It is unclear. "Prices can appropriately rise in those industries where the increase of productivity is smaller than the national trend"—but rise by how much? "Prices should fall in those industries where the increase of productivity exceeds the national trend"—but fall by how much? The historical facts presented in Chapter IX do not support the notion that percentage changes in relative prices should be exactly equal (and of opposite sign) to percentage changes in relative labor productivity—if that is what is supposed to be read into the guidepost.

A second point relates to the exceptions. In Chapter IX we saw that even in the long run factors other than labor productivity influence price and that as a group these factors are as important as productivity. Over shorter periods of time, the other factors usually exercise an even greater influence on prices than does productivity. This raises a question about exceptions. Can we effectively limit the number of exceptions to the general productivity guidepost? This question is important, for if guideposts are to be practicable, they must be subject to relatively few exceptions.

Since exceptions would in any case be unavoidable in the complex economy in which we live, we must then ask what sort of rules we can use to govern exceptions. These must be simple and clear if they are to work at all. However, the factors (other than productivity) that create the need for exceptions are many, and they differ in relative importance from industry to industry and from time to time. It is not easy to prescribe clear and simple rules to govern exceptions. Nor did the council succeed in doing so.

Third, the price guidepost ignores, as does the wage guidepost, the fact that general price levels have not remained constant. Whatever may be said about appropriate price changes in a noninflationary economy in which there is "observance of the guideposts" must be qualified when wholesale prices move up at the rate of 2 percent per annum, as they have since 1964.

Finally, there is a serious doubt whether the statistical information needed to apply the price guideposts is adequate. What is needed, of course, is not simply a single national index of productivity, as in the case of wages, but a full array of separate indexes, one for each industry. But all the available statistics are rough, and for many industries even poor quantitative information is entirely lacking.

Even when the deficiencies of the wage and price guideposts are admitted, one might argue that they provide a useful, if rough, guide for which no better substitute is available.

It is doubtful, however, that the economy would run

better with than without the guideposts. Although adherence to the guideposts—if it could be secured—would serve to lessen the rate of inflation, other consequences would be less desirable. Indeed, strict adherence to the guideposts would be tantamount to price and wage fixing by government. This would tend to throttle competition, impede the movement of resources into new and desirable uses, diminish incentives to economize in the use of scarce resources, and replace the price system with less desirable ways of rationing goods or services in short supply. In a word, the incentives that lead to investment in labor quality, to investment in tangible capital, and to improvements in efficiency—that is, to an increase in labor productivity—would be weakened.

But the guideposts are, in fact, impractical instruments of policy. They cannot do the work they are supposed to do when expansive monetary and fiscal policies are being followed to stimulate demand. When the consumer price index is rising, when the workers in industries where pressure has been applied to observe the guideposts see larger wage increases occurring in other industries, when employers compete vigorously for labor in a situation approaching full employment—when these things happen as a result of an expansive monetary and fiscal policy, our own experience and the experience in Europe suggests that exhortation to conform to the guideposts loses its effectiveness. Most of us have a limited capacity to place our own interests second to those of the public at large, and this is especially the case when there are differences of opinion as to whether the public's interests would in fact be served by the sacrifice.

It was no great surprise, therefore, when the new Administration announced—at the first Presidential press conference in 1969—that it did not "go along with the suggestion that inflation can be effectively controlled by exhorting labor and management and industry to follow certain guidelines."

To prevent inflation, it is better to depend on appropriate monetary and fiscal policy. To find jobs for workers who remain unemployed, once a sustainable level of prosperity has been reached, it is better to develop a more effective program of training or retraining, of improved labor intelligence, and of still other "structural" improvements. To avoid the undesirable effects on wages and prices of excessive market power, the solution is to hammer away at the sources of this excessive power. To eliminate the floors that hold some prices and wages above economically sound levels, the government supports under the floors must be removed. To satisfy the expectations of workers for higher incomes, appropriate policies to raise labor productivity should be adopted and vigorously pursued.

CHAPTER XII

Policies to Raise Productivity

There is so much talk, these days, of the responsibilities of government for this and for that, that many of us have forgotten a fundamental fact: The main sources of increase in the productivity of labor are, by far, actions by individuals in pursuit of their private interests. It is to improve their own knowledge that students spend their time and energy and their parents' money on education. It is to add to their own capital that families and corporations save. And they seek ways to increase the efficiency with which their labor and capital are used in order to get more for themselves.

Sometimes, however, these private efforts will not or cannot go far enough. Opportunities to raise productivity that are highly profitable from a *social* point of view will not be seized when they pay too little from a *private* point of view. The benefits from research in basic science or even technology, for example, may not be fully captured by the individuals or companies making the effort and bearing the costs. There will then be less

investment in research than there "ought" to be. Or
social arrangements that may have had merit in the
past—ancient systems of land tenure or of taxation—
may now be dulling private incentives to raise productivity. Or monopolistic barriers to the application of
new methods may be raising the costs of innovation or
reducing the private return one may reasonably expect
from innovation.

Sometimes, also, these private efforts will go too far.
Advantageous though they might be to the individual
or firm, they could be adding little or nothing, or even
tending to reduce, the nation's productivity. This will
be the case when public support of certain industries is
excessive, as many economists believe is true of agriculture. Or, to take a less controversial example, an industry may cut its own costs and raise its own productivity
but do so by using technologies that pollute rivers and
tend to reduce the productivity of communities down-
stream.

When the pursuit of private interests falls short or
goes too far, to judge by a social (rather than a private)
accounting of the results, the government's responsibility is clear and it must take action. The government can
attempt to raise productivity by removing obstacles to
private enterprise, that is, by *freeing* private enterprise.
It can support, or support more strongly, private activities that yield greater social than private rates of
return. It can reduce or eliminate its support of private
activities that yield smaller social than private rates of
return or even frown on such activities when this appears necessary.

When stated in these general terms, almost everybody
would agree on the desirability and kind of govern-

mental policies to raise productivity. But it is easier to agree on general principles than on specific applications. The sources of productivity increase listed in earlier chapters constitute only the headings in a program. If it is to be useful, a program must specify just what should be done, how to do it, what cost (in terms of current consumption or other national objectives) is likely to be incurred, and what returns may be expected.

There will be differences of opinion on each of these specifications and therefore on what to pick out of the "menu of choices," to use Edward Denison's expressive phrase, that are available to increase productivity.

In part, disagreement will arise because opinions differ on what would be most effective. We simply lack the knowledge that would point clearly to the best among several possible policies. We do know a lot more than we used to know about the sources of economic growth and about the current developments that government should be prepared to encourage or to resist. But we do not know nearly as much as is needed to turn the problem of economic policy into the kind of technical problem that confronts engineers when they build bridges.

We are not certain, for example, what an additional tax dollar invested in elementary education would yield in higher national productivity as compared with what that dollar would yield if invested in higher education, or in education as compared with roads, or in roads as compared with antitrust or antidiscrimination enforcement; or what the dollar would yield if taxes were not raised and the dollar were left in private hands. Even when we are pretty sure that another dollar (or million dollars) would raise productivity most effectively if invested in education, we may have doubts about investing a second dollar (or million dollars), for expenditure in any direction usually encounters the "law of diminishing returns." We may believe that mergers tend to reduce competition and thus to discourage innovation, but we may also believe that large firms are better able to invest in the risky business of research and development, and we may therefore be uncertain just when the social advantages of a merger are offset by its social disadvantages.

What all this means is that it is difficult to determine the benefits that will result from following a particular policy and what that policy will cost.

Differences of opinion on policy will arise also because growth of productivity is not the only national objective. Our people want high-level consumption today, as well as tomorrow, and also reasonably full employment, equity in the distribution of income, economic stability, and freedom. These various objectives are valued differently by different citizens. To get more productivity, some would pay a higher price in the form of regulations and restrictions on economic freedom, for example, than would others—even if all agreed, which is doubtful, what the price was. To reduce current unemployment, some would be more willing than others to tolerate a "little" inefficiency and a slower rate of increase in productivity, if this were the cost. These differences in the values that people put on various national objectives are important, because virtually everything the government does, or could do, tends to favor some objectives more than others.

Finally, and not least important in the political arena where national policy is set, are the differences in policy that will arise from differences in sectional interests. Despite a net advantage to society as a whole, some groups might suffer a disadvantage from a particular proposal to raise national productivity, such as reducing tariffs or farm price supports, and they will resist it. Even when all would gain, there may be differences on what to do if some would gain more than others.

Of course, differences of opinion do get resolved in the political arena. But as long as differences exist, any economic program is first of all a subject for debate and study, rather than a prescription ready to be filled by a technical staff of economists and lawyers.

In the present context, then, what seems worth presenting is not anyone's list of pet ideas, but rather illustrations of the kinds of suggestions for governmental action that have appeared in a variety of respectable sources, public and private.

Suggestions have been made for government action on each one of the factors that determine labor productivity—the factors that affect the quality of labor, the volume of tangible capital, and the efficiency with which labor and capital are used. Some are proposals for more and some for less governmental expenditure or regulation, or for more expenditure or regulation in one direction and less in another. Some proposals suggest governmental ownership and operation, some suggest governmental ownership and private operation, and some prefer government subsidy or other encouragement of entirely private ownership and operation. Some are very broad in scope, and some quite narrow.

To be more specific, consider proposals to raise the quality of labor. The major emphasis, these days, is on governmental support of education. But suggestions can also be, and have been, made to permit the immigration of larger numbers of highly qualified foreign workers, many of whom are kept out by restrictive quotas. It is sometimes argued, as well, that a shorter workweek would pay for itself by raising labor productivity—even in the United States of today when hours of work are already fewer than in most other countries. And the same kind of argument is used by proponents of improved and subsidized health services, though it is only fair to say that their objective is more humanitarian than economic.

As for education, suggestions for strengthening our school systems may underscore the need for more public schools (at all levels) or—following Adam Smith, who believed competition for students made for better teaching—the emphasis may be on the support of private schools, among which students could choose freely. Most frequently, additional per capita expenditures by government are proposed, but sometimes the emphasis is on the redirection of the present, supposedly inefficient, distribution of expenditures. When the support of private schools is in question, the proposals may be for government funds, or they may suggest indirect subsidy through favorable (or more favorable) tax treatment of family expenditures on education and of philanthropic contributions to educational institutions. And there are any number of proposals for widening and improving on-the-job training and retraining to be supported by government.

To increase the volume of tangible capital—another major source of higher labor productivity—some proposals have aimed at strengthening private incentives to save and invest. For example, the taxation of personal consumption, rather than personal income, has been proposed in order to encourage private saving. In recent years, attention has been focused on higher depreciation rates, investment credits, and other allowances in the calculation of taxable business income to encourage private investment.

Stress has also been placed on government's responsibility to build up the nation's roads, airports, waterways, power supplies, urban water, sewage, and other utilities, and other forms of "social overhead capital." The term, "infrastructure," has been coined to describe the kind of facility for which government's responsibility is especially great. There are, however, differences of opinion on just how the facilities are to be financed and who is to manage them.

Proposals to raise efficiency in the use of labor and capital are illustrated by the recent "Kennedy round." In this series of negotiations, the federal government worked with many other national governments to reduce the tariffs that limit the scale of markets and thus the division of labor. There is already under way a discussion of a reduction of quotas also and of other non-tariff barriers to international trade.

Government support of research and the dissemination of research findings provide another illustration. This support has already reached a high level in this country but still more funds are being sought, as are longer-term commitments to reduce the waste caused by the uncertainty of future support. Where too much is being attempted, as some believe to be the case in space and medical research, proposals are being made to shift the funds to other subjects.

Of still other proposals, some of which overlap the three classes of factors we have distinguished, we can list only a few:

Updating of public policies on local transportation to lessen congestion in our city streets, which can mean changes in policies regarding on-street parking, investment in municipal garages, imposition of regulations requiring off-street unloading, strengthening of commuter railroads and bus lines, and still other policies, including policies regarding user charges;

Efforts to lessen racial and other discrimination with more or stronger legislation and education;

A reduction of legislative protection of featherbedding and other restrictive work practices, and substitution of more socially desirable ways of protecting labor from the harsher effects of technological change;

A modernization of obsolete local building codes that interfere with the introduction of more economical materials and methods;

A search for ways to lessen labor and industry monopoly power without unduly weakening the socially desirable functions of labor unions or doing serious damage to the economies that large-scale production may yield;

Elimination of resale price maintenance and other forms of legislation that tend to lessen competition;

Reform of the farm program and other subsidy programs that divert resources into uneconomical areas of production; and where subsidies are desirable, make them open and subject to regular and frequent reconsideration;

Aid to smaller firms to increase their efficiency by setting up productivity councils such as exist in several European countries;

Encouragement of further consolidation of local governments and of firms in regulated industries, when this would reduce costs and improve services;

Improvement of the allocation of labor by lessening or removing the inhibiting effects that pension systems and other forms of protection may have on the mobility of labor;

Improvement of economic statistics and the other forms of economic intelligence useful to workers, consumers, businessmen, and government officials.

It is obvious that a suggestion to seek "ways to lessen labor and industry monopoly power, without unduly weakening the socially desirable functions" of labor organizations and large-scale productive units, must entail much study and discussion before it can lead to a concrete proposal that would be widely acceptable. But this is true of every one of the preceding suggestions— even the simple suggestion to modernize obsolete building codes, as the following story tells.

Early in 1966 the Advisory Commission on Intergovernmental Relations issued a detailed report on building codes. The document noted that the "chaos and confusion of hundreds of conflicting local building codes" were costing home buyers an average of at least a thousand dollars a house. At an annual rate of construction of something like a million and a half housing units, this meant at least a billion and a half dollars each year. The excessive cost reflected a compound of unnecessary requirements in the codes and unnecessary diversity among them in those requirements that do make sense. In the case of the Cleveland metropolitan area, for example, a contractor wanting to operate throughout the area might have to contend with no less than fifty different building codes.

After eighty pages or so of discussion, the report of the commission concluded with about a dozen recommendations. However, many of these were not recommendations on ways of changing the codes. Rather, they recommended that research be undertaken on building methods and on codes and that a model code—which does not now exist—be developed. And, as a further illustration of how widely opinions may differ, a number of members of the commission questioned whether the time was ripe even for these recommendations!

The suggestions listed above constitute only a small sample of what economists and other people are thinking about. But rather than add to it or speculate about what inventive minds may put forward in the future, let us conclude with some general rules for sound policy.

Most important, increases in productivity depend primarily on private investment in training and education, in plant and equipment, and in the search for means of raising efficiency. This being the case, it is desirable that as far as possible every piece of legislation and every administrative action, whatever its primary objectives and whether they be of long- or short-range character, should—in Arthur F. Burns's words—"encourage consumers and businessmen to look with hope and confidence to their own and the country's future."

Nor should we forget that too little is yet known about the connection between any given policy and its results. This being the case, it is desirable that policy be kept flexible. At the same time, however, shifts in policy should not be so erratic as to create uncertainty and thereby discourage private plans and actions for raising productivity.

Limitations on our knowledge also suggest the importance of experimenting with new ideas on a modest scale. This requires holding open the possibility of retreat, which in turn requires that commitments to keep unsuccessful experiments alive be avoided. It follows, also, that every experiment should provide for prompt and reliable feedback of information on the costs and benefits of the experimental policy—information to be weighed not by those who may have developed a vested interest in the experiment but by persons who can be objective.

A final point: Policy must proceed on a wide front.

To try to raise productivity by concentrating attention on just one of the factors or groups of factors that affect productivity—on plant and equipment, if that happens to be the fashion, or on education, or on research and development—would be wasteful. It would be just as foolish to try to stimulate private efforts to raise productivity by using only one of the means available to government—tax policy, financial support, or regulation. No government can afford to neglect any of the sources of productivity increase or overlook the possibilities of tapping them with any of the means at its command.

PART V

Productivity Abroad

CHAPTER XIII

Productivity Differences among Countries

Pan Am Flight Number 1, or the equivalent on another of the great international airlines, will take you on a quick trip around the world. If you make the usual stops on what has become the present-day Grand Tour, you'll probably put down not only in London, Paris, and Rome but also in Cairo or Istanbul, Teheran, Karachi, New Delhi or Calcutta, Bangkok, Hong Kong, and Tokyo, before you head home for Honolulu and "the States."

In each of the great cities you visit, keep your eyes and ears—and nose—open as you are driven from the airport to your hotel. Walk around a bit, even if only "downtown." Take a trolley or bus away from the center and stretch your legs at the end of the line before returning to your hotel. Note the look of the people—don't miss the children—the clothes they wear and don't wear, the homes they live in, the food they buy and eat, and the merchandise on display in the shops and stands. Don't hesitate to peek in—discreetly, of course, and with a smile—at any small factory or crafts-man's shop you may come across. When you get a chance, ask about the wages the average unskilled worker gets per day. (The concierge in your hotel will be able to tell you about this, though he'll be puzzled as to why you want to know.) Watch the traffic in the streets and see how goods and people are transported—in what kinds of vehicles and with what sources of power.

On your way into town, how were the roads? Perhaps you got a glimpse of a few farms. What were the build-ings like, the animals, the equipment? Who was doing the sowing, tilling, or harvesting, and how? Surely there are some buildings under construction along the road or in town. How are they being put up—what workers, tools, materials, and equipment, and at what pace?

Of course, all this will supply little direct information on the situation in the hinterland areas and at best can provide only a small sample of how things are even in the cities visited. Yet what you can see, hear, smell, and feel in this way will make believable to you differences in productivity levels that would otherwise be very much harder to accept.

For few Americans quite realize how extraordinarily high the United States level of labor productivity is, compared with the level of most other countries. The rest of the world is so far below us in this regard that an hour of a man's labor yields, on the average, less than a tenth the output obtained in this country. In terms of its money value, the average hourly output outside the United States is worth 50 cents or less, measured in recent (1967) prices. Inside the United States, it is over five dollars. With labor productivity growing in the United States by about 3 percent per year, this means that the average output obtained per man-hour in the rest of the world today is no more than what we *add* to our output per man-hour in just three ordinary years.

These striking conclusions deserve close examination. Let us start by viewing them against the background of international differences in output per capita and in the work done per capita.

Suppose we rank the hundred-odd countries of the world, including those on the other side of the iron and bamboo curtains, in order of level of national output per capita in a recent year. (The ranking can hardly be precise, as we will see later, but it is good enough for our purpose.)

As we would expect, the United States stands at the head of the line, with a per capita output of about $4,000 of 1967 purchasing power. Canada, New Zealand, and the more prosperous western European countries are next in order, with levels of output per capita ranging between one-half and two-thirds of ours. Other European countries follow with levels ranging down from one half to something like a seventh of ours, or $500 to $600 per capita per year. The Soviet Union stands somewhere near half the U.S. mark, with a per capita output of about $1,800, plus or minus a few hundred, and Japan, perhaps a little below the Soviet Union. The rest of the world's countries, with few exceptions, are all below the $400 level. Most of them, in fact, produced under $250 of goods and services per capita. At the very tail end of the line, with a per capita output of $100 per annum, or even less, are the heavily populated Asian countries, including India, Pakistan,

Indonesia, and mainland China, as well as many of the new African countries.

With these figures before us, it is hardly necessary to ask whether the richer countries rank high in output per capita because more or harder work is done per capita than in the poorer countries. In the light of the huge disparities in per capita output levels, it is obvious what the answer must be. The differences in per capita output—and the real incomes that go along with output—cannot conceivably be explained by anything but huge differences in labor productivity.

Indeed, all the available information indicates that international differences in labor productivity are even bigger than those in output per capita. The poor countries make more use of child labor. They put in longer hours. Their work is more back-breaking than the work in rich countries. In a word, they do more work per capita, not less. This conclusion may be contrary to the impression of some Westerners that there is much lazing about in the poor countries they visit. But the visitors may simply be misinterpreting adaptations to climatic conditions—siesta habits, for example—or failing to understand the effects of inadequate food and poor health on the effort than can be sustained.

In any case, the differences among countries in the number of man-hours of work done per capita are small compared with the differences in output per capita. Even if work per capita were positively correlated with output per capita, rather than inversely, by far the more important source of differences in output per capita would still have to be labor productivity. Productivity is *the* factor accounting for per capita output differences across the earth.

Indeed, differences in labor productivity are so great that some countries with larger populations produce in the aggregate no more than other countries with small populations. The national product of Communist China, the most heavily populated country on earth with something like 800 million inhabitants, has been exceeded in recent years by the national product of each of four western European countries with populations of only 50 million each—the United Kingdom, France, West Germany, and even Italy. Pakistan, with a population close to 100 million, has a national product substantially less than little Switzerland, with a population one twentieth as large.

A comparison of American-Russian productivity levels is worth giving in some detail, not only because there is much interest in it here and abroad, but also because it illustrates the ambiguities in these international comparisons. (The year 1960 is the most recent for which the analysis has been made outside Russia. The calculations by the Russians themselves are of little value for our purpose.)

The national product of the U.S.S.R. in 1960 ranged from about a third to two thirds of the national product of the United States. A difference must be expected because the great variety of products that make up a nation's output can be aggregated and the total compared with the output of another country only by using a set of relative values for the various products. As in every comparison, there are two sets of relative values —in this case, an American and a Russian. These differ very widely. When relative dollar prices in the United States are used, the Russian level of output turns out to be two thirds of that of the United States. When relative ruble prices in Russia are used, the level of Russian output is reduced to one third of the American.

In addition to the more usual reasons given in Chapter I, such as differences in tastes and resources, peculiarities of the Communist price system help to account for the differences in relative values. Steel and other commodities needed to speed up industrialization are heavily subsidized in Russia, and their prices are thus kept relatively low. Consumer commodities, such as automobiles, are priced very high there in order to discourage their purchase. As a result, the commodities that bulk large in Russian output have relatively low ruble prices but relatively high dollar prices; conversely, the commodities that bulk small in Russian output have relatively high ruble prices and relatively low dollar prices.

In contrast to the low level of Russian output, compared with the American, the level of Russian labor input—man-hours of work done—was high in 1960. For one thing, the population was somewhat larger in the U.S.S.R. than in the United States, by 15 or 20 percent. The percentage of the population in the labor force also was larger, in this case by 20 or 30 percent, because a larger fraction of the women and of the boys and old men were at work there. Finally, weekly hours of labor in Russia were longer—closer to forty-five or fifty hours as compared with forty in the United States.

It follows, then, that whereas output in Russia ranged from a third to two thirds of output in the United States, output per man-hour was even lower—between something like a fourth to somewhat under a half of the United States level. The gap has been narrowed since 1960, but it still remains wide.

We should not forget, however, that Russia's productivity is much higher than that in most other parts of the world, even though it is lower than that of the United States and western Europe. It is for this reason, as well as because it is a large country that devotes a better than average fraction of its output to building and maintaining its military and political power, that Russia is the world's mightiest nation, next to the United States.

Before we go on to see how countries have differed in rates of productivity change, let us turn to a little problem that we slighted at the beginning of this chapter.

The problem crops up when we ask what the average level of labor productivity is outside the United States. With so wide a range in the national levels of labor productivity, and with so heavy a concentration of the earth's population in the countries of very low productivity, the answer is sensitive to just how the average is calculated.

If we were to array all the workers outside the United States in order of labor productivity level, walk down the line until we reached the man at the middle, and pick him as representative of the average outside our borders, the hourly productivity of this man—the median worker—would be only about 25 cents in 1967.

Only when we add up the world's annual output of about $1,500 billion (excluding the output of the United States) and divide the total by the three or four trillion hours of work done per year by the world's one and a half billion workers, do we get the average of 50 cents or less mentioned earlier. That estimate seemed low enough to startle the reader, and I thought I had better not shock him with anything lower.

Some part of the present-day differences among nations in levels of labor productivity results from differences in long-term rates of growth of labor productivity. This does not necessarily mean, however, that labor productivity has declined in some countries and gone up in others.

What is known of trends over the last hundred years or so points to a remarkably general rise in output per man-hour. This is certainly true of all countries—mostly today's developed countries—for which reasonably accurate estimates are available for a half century or more. We cannot be so sure about the decades of the nineteenth century, when the statistical records even of the developed countries thin out. Yet for all countries, even the poorer, there are bits of statistical information, as well as information on the sources and the fruits of higher labor productivity. This direct and indirect evidence suggests that today's productivity levels are above those of a century ago in virtually all countries. The exceptions, if any, are likely to be countries now in the throes of war or social upheaval. In that case, of course, what we see is not a downward trend but rather a downward deviation from an upward trend.

But although all countries have probably raised their labor productivity levels over the past century, the rates of advance have been highly varied. Most of the countries for which statistical estimates are available for a sufficiently long period fall in the range between 1.5 and 2.5 percent per annum. None of the estimates are higher than about 2.5—the United States experienced a rate close to this top figure—and only a few are lower than 1.5, with none much below 1 percent. However, as already mentioned, this sample of rates of growth in national labor productivity is bound to overstate the more general experience because it relates largely to the developed countries. Most other countries undoubtedly experienced lower rates of increase in labor productivity over the century taken as a whole. It is reasonable on the basis of the available information to suppose that the range of rates of increase that would include virtually all the countries of the world is between, say, 0.5 percent (the figure for India) and 2.5 (the figure for Sweden). This range is wide indeed. Compounded over a century, it means the difference between a modest rise to about two thirds above the starting level at one extreme, and an increase to as much as eleven times the starting level at the other.

Unfortunately, most of the countries with low rates of increase in productivity during the past century—India is again the example—had low levels of productivity to begin with. Although the labor of every country, or virtually every country, is more productive today than a century ago, the richer countries have done better in raising their capacity to produce than the poorer countries.

This fact has a profound significance. It means that the international productivity gap between the developed and the developing countries widened—rather than narrowed—and widened relatively as well as absolutely.

Even if little or no improvement had taken place in a few sections of the world, it is safe to say that the average level of labor productivity of mankind as a whole has risen substantially.

The world average has been pushed up not only by the increases in individual countries but also by the more rapid growth of population over the century as a whole—though not in the recent period—in countries with high initial levels of output per man-hour. Taking this important fact into account we may put the average rate of increase in the productivity of all human labor during the past century at something over 1 percent per annum, and maybe closer to 1.5 than to 1. If this estimate of the change is near the mark, it indicates that the average level of productivity outside the United States a hundred years ago was in the vicinity of 15 cents per hour in terms of recent purchasing power, compared with the 50 cents mentioned earlier.

Although all these estimates are rough, and at best indicative only of orders of magnitude, we can be pretty sure of three things:

First, even a 1 percent rise in labor productivity per annum is far higher than the average rate of increase that must have been experienced since man's appearance on earth.

Second, a 1 percent rate of increase is higher than the corresponding rate of increase in the aggregate amount of work done. The population of the earth has grown by less than 1 percent per annum over the century as a whole, and man-hours worked per capita have probably fallen somewhat, as hours were reduced. It follows that men today produce far more than did men a century ago not only because there are many more men but, even more important, because men today are able to get more from an hour of their labor than were their grandfathers or great-grandfathers.

Third, even the top figure of about a 2.5 percent rise in labor productivity per annum—a rate sustained over a period as long as fifty to a hundred years only in the United States, Sweden, and perhaps Japan and one or two other countries—is less than the rate of increase that most countries of the world now hope, expect, and assume in their plans for economic growth.

As in the United States, the upward march of labor productivity in other countries has often been speeded up and has as often been slowed down, sometimes to the point of declining absolutely for a time.

Among the sources of these fluctuations have been the weather, which has put a visible mark on national output per man-hour in countries in which agriculture is important. Russia, mainland China, and India are outstanding recent examples. Business cycles have been of importance in industrialized countries, as the earlier discussion in Chapter VII indicated. Centrally planned economies have escaped business cycles, but not the consequences of poor central planning. The ill-fated "great leap forward" in China, for example, made economic (and other) conditions visibly worse rather than better. And the catastrophes of war and political and social upheaval, not altogether separate from the other sources of instability, continue to plague mankind.

Wars and social disorders have been less frequent than crop cycles, business cycles, or central-planning errors—though the present generation of men seems to be suffering another high in the frequency of wars and social disorder. But even if less frequent, their effects have usually been more violent and more prolonged. They have caused disorganization, undermaintenance and destruction of plant and equipment, and the loss or diversion of trained personnel. These have cut labor productivity, sometimes drastically. During recovery, once peace and stability have been established, labor productivity has often risen at an exceptionally rapid pace. But this high rate has not always continued long enough to bring productivity up to the level it would have reached had the troubles been avoided.

The period following World War II may prove to be exceptional in this regard. In most countries, as in the United States, the recent period has witnessed higher rates of growth in labor productivity than those found in the long-term averages. Even after about 1952, when most of the immediate effects of World War II had probably been overcome, labor productivity continued to advance at annual rates that appear high by historical standards.

Undoubtedly, it is their favorable postwar experience that has encouraged countries to expect as high—or even higher—rates in the years ahead also. Whether these expectations will be justified remains to be seen. What happens will surely depend, apart from luck, on how much the countries are willing to do to strengthen the factors that determine labor productivity, and how wisely they make and implement their plans for economic development.

Success in dealing with the problem of population growth will be an especially important factor in many of the poorer countries. While their average annual rate of population growth was below that of the richer countries during the past century considered as a whole, the reverse has been the case since the end of World War II. Population has been growing with exceptional rapidity in the poorer countries.

This burst of population in these countries has tended to hold back the average rate of increase of labor productivity for mankind as a whole. Indeed, it is quite possible that during the postwar period the world's average level of productivity rose *less* rapidly than during the seven or eight decades before the war.

CHAPTER XIV

Explaining the International Productivity Gap

The causes of international differences in levels of labor productivity are clearly visible in many forms. Differences in quality of labor? Our world traveler will easily recognize low levels of education—not, to be sure, because natives fail to understand English, but because children are helping with his luggage or clearing the dishes from his table at an age when they would be in school in the United States. Differences in volume of tangible capital per worker? Among the "sights" in Lima are the broken-down taxis and in Taiwan the pedicabs. Differences in the efficiency with which labor and capital are used? Another "sight" is the cattle obstructing street traffic in Calcutta. And felt rather than seen are the red tape and *mañana* in some capitals, not all Spanish-speaking.

But observation can only be suggestive. To weigh the factors determining the labor productivity of a country and compare them with those in the United States, we need to know much more than even a trained observer could tell after a visit.

For some countries we do know, because economists have taken the trouble to sift and analyze the relevant statistics and make the necessary comparisons. In the Italy of 1960, for example, output per man-hour was about 65 percent below the American level, according to Edward Denison's careful comparison. Differences in educational levels, he estimated, accounted for nearly 10 percentage points of the difference in productivity; differences in tangible capital per worker, for another 15; and for the other 40, differences in the efficiency with which labor and capital are used.

It is interesting that all three groups of factors point in the same direction. Italy is below the United States in labor quality, capital quantity, and efficiency. As interesting is the fact that of the three sources of difference in labor productivity the largest is efficiency. This was also the case, the reader will recall, for the sources of increase in the labor productivity of the United States. Is this generally true over space and time? Before we answer this question, let us take a closer look at each of the three main sources of international differences in levels and rates of change in labor productivity.

In all countries, some of the wealth in human capital is derived from investment in education. The amounts invested per worker vary enormously, however, partly because income levels differ and partly because of differences in the fraction of income devoted to this form of investment. In general, the stock of educational capital per worker abroad is less than in the United States, with the lowest levels of education in the least productive countries.

To determine the amount of education, we must first take account of the number of years or days of school attendance. Thus, in the United States, the average number of years of education in 1962 was about eleven, but the average in Italy was only half that level. Allowance must also be made for the greater value of secondary and collegiate education as compared with primary schooling, which further widens the difference in educational capital per worker.

Calculations of this kind have been made only for a few countries. For most, we must judge the situation from the literacy rate. Until recently, for example, less than a quarter of the population aged 15 and over in India, Pakistan, and Iran were able to read and write.

Although the available measurements are very crude, it is clear that education is generally an important factor in accounting for contemporary differences in productivity levels.

The contribution of education to changes in labor productivity over time is also important. As has the United States, other countries have increased their investments in educational capital per worker, but the rates of increase have varied. During the post-World War II period, for example, the rate of increase in the United States was more rapid than in northwestern Europe. With educational capital per worker smaller in Europe than in the United States when the war ended and growing less rapidly since then, we have here a source of widening rather than narrowing of the productivity gap between the United States and Europe.

In addition to levels of education, other aspects of

labor quality play a part in explaining the productivity gap, especially between the high- and the low-income countries. In poor countries a larger proportion of the labor force consists of children, who cannot be as productive as adults. Also, the workers in these countries are generally fed less adequately. Manioc, for example, so prominent in the diet of some poor countries because it is a cheap belly-filler, lacks protein. And health is not as good or as well protected as in rich countries. Natives as well as tourists suffer from "the traveler's ailment."

Some readers might also want to include among the factors making for differences in labor quality the innate intellectual capacity of a country's labor force. Whether there are such innate differences among nations is still a moot question, however, at least scientifically. Even if the differences are at all significant, it is pretty clear that their effects on the quality of labor are small compared with the effects of education and age and food and the other factors affecting health. No doubt, individuals vary widely in intellect, but it is safe to say that the variation among national *averages* is far less than the variation among *individuals*. It is with these national averages that we are concerned.

Besides its educational capital, every country also has a substantial amount of tangible capital—real capital assets—that it uses in production, and with the assistance of which its labor productivity is higher than it could otherwise be. Again, as with educational capital, every country for which we have some sort of estimate —and probably every other country as well—has over the years increased its stock of tangible capital and done so more rapidly than it has increased its labor force or the man-hours they work. Everywhere, then, labor productivity has been pushed up by increase in tangible capital per man-hour.

As we all know, whether we have taken that Pan Am trip or not, the quantity of tangible capital per man-hour varies enormously around the globe. In the United States, for example, hardly anyone lifts or carries heavy weights any more. Fork trucks, elevators, derricks, hay-loaders, bulldozers, and motor trucks—more tangible capital—shoulder the burdens. These substitutes for human labor are also used in other countries but not nearly in such large volume.

The amount of equipment and other capital per man-hour drops as one moves from countries with high output per man-hour to countries with low. In 1960, tangible capital per man-hour in the United Kingdom was half that of the United States. In Italy, it was slightly over one fourth. And, in India, where half the tangible capital is still in land (the proportion in land generally declines as a country's wealth increases), the amount of tangible capital per man-hour may be only around 2 percent of the United States level. Low levels of productivity are associated with a scarcity of tangible as well as intangible capital.

As a comparison of the preceding figures with those given in Chapter XIII suggests, capital-output ratios vary within a very narrow range, compared with labor-output ratios. For this reason, a useful first approximation to an index of the amount of capital per worker in a country is provided by its output per man-hour. This appears to be true also of change over time, when allowance is made for the tendency noted in Chapter V —and apparent in the records of countries generally— for national capital-output ratios to trend downward.

These downward trends in capital-output ratios mean that capital per man-hour has generally risen somewhat less rapidly than output per man-hour. It means also that, like trends in productivity, trends in capital per man-hour have been highly varied. In northwestern Europe, for example, tangible capital per man-hour rose more rapidly than in the United States during 1955–62. This speedier increase in tangible capital helped to offset the slower increase in educational capital noted earlier.

It is interesting that the increase in capital per man-hour in northwestern Europe was concentrated in non-residential structures, business and governmental equipment, and business inventories. The quantity of capital invested in dwellings, per worker, rose more rapidly in the United States than in Europe. The higher rate of growth of productivity in Europe does not necessarily mean that the United States must have invested too much in housing and not enough in business plant and equipment. It is possible, of course, that the United States government, by subsidy, tax policy, and otherwise, encouraged private investors to make housing investments that were excessive from a social viewpoint; or that these investors made serious mistakes and invested what from a private viewpoint was too much. But it would take more than the figure cited to support either of these possible conclusions. For it is also possible, and on general grounds rather more reasonable, to presume that prospective social and private rates of return in the United States and in Europe differed in such a way as to justify the difference in the distribution of investment between housing and other capital assets.

A rather different point also deserves a comment.

What counts, when one asks about the contribution of capital to increase in labor productivity, is not capital by itself. It is capital per worker or per man-hour. When population growth, and therefore also growth in the labor force, is very rapid—as it is these days in the less developed countries—even a high rate of savings may mean only a small rate of growth in capital per worker.

Efficiency in the use of labor and capital, measured by output per unit of labor and capital, is our third source of labor productivity. As we saw in earlier chapters, it covers a number of factors—the quantity and quality of technology and other knowledge applied in the process of production, the degree of specialization permitted by the scale of markets, the effects of the length of the workday or workweek on the intensity of labor, and the way in which economic organization and policy and political and cultural factors distort (or improve) the allocation of resources to different uses.

Countries vary among themselves and also change over time in all these respects. Some of this variation is a consequence of differences in levels or growth rates of income per capita. The obvious examples, shorter hours of labor and bigger scale of markets, also illustrate how an increase in labor productivity tends to generate its own further increase. Some of the variation reflects the accidents of history—for example, in setting national borders and thus making the scale of markets wide or narrow. Some reflects the values put on national objectives other than economic growth, values that influence economic policy and make for more or less efficiency in the use of resources.

But, whatever the reasons, the variation in the factors affecting efficiency is great, and the outcome—the net balance, for some of these factors tend to raise and some to lower efficiency—is revealed by very considerable international differences in levels and in rates of change of output per unit of labor and capital.

All countries are more efficient in this sense than they were in earlier generations. Useful knowledge has increased everywhere, markets have generally expanded, and cuts in hours have been fairly universal. It is more difficult to make a general statement about the other factors. What we call economic policy, for example, is a complex of various policies, not all consistent, and its changes and effects are not easily summarized. But even when policy has, on net balance, tended to depress labor productivity, it has not as a rule been sufficiently powerful to offset the other, favorable, factors.

Not all countries are equally efficient, however, nor have they all increased their efficiency by equal percentages. As in the case of the other main sources of labor productivity, levels of productivity and of efficiency and corresponding rates of change are found to be correlated. This is not surprising, if only because higher efficiency is so important a source of higher labor productivity.

Indeed, as the discussion to this point has already suggested, of the three sources of labor productivity, efficiency is in many cases—perhaps most—the major factor accounting for international differences in rates of increase in labor productivity.

This may be the most striking lesson learned from the measurements of output per unit of labor and capital, to judge by the surprise expressed by many economists when they first saw them. Between 1928 and 1948, under the influence of empirical work with the so-called "production function," which expresses in

mathematical form the relationship between output on
the one hand and labor and capital input on the other,
it was believed that an increase in labor productivity,
as well as international differences in labor productivity, could be explained very largely by differences in
the amount of tangible capital available per man-hour.
We know better now. Additions to, and improvements
in, our statistical information during the past two decades have made it clear that quality of labor is also a
significant factor. We have learned, further, that even
the combination of better labor quality and more tangible capital is insufficient to explain higher output per
man-hour. In the United States, as we have seen, as
much as two thirds of the 2.4 percent average annual
increase in output per man-hour since 1889 is accounted
for by the increase in efficiency. Corresponding calculations for a few other countries available for periods of
up to five decades and for additional countries for the
last fifteen or twenty years yield roughly similar results.

It is noteworthy, also, that in virtually all cases, at
least as far as trends are concerned, the three factors
have worked together. All have made for higher labor
productivity. To return to the questions posed at the
opening of the chapter, what we noticed in the comparison of the United States and Italy is *generally* the case:
labor productivity is higher everywhere because everywhere the quality of labor has improved, the quantity
of capital per worker has grown, and efficiency in the
use of labor and capital is higher.

Can we be more specific about the relative importance
of the several factors subsumed under the heading of
efficiency? We can—if we are willing to entertain estimates based more on judgment than on hard facts. But

the judgment of an economist as knowledgeable as Edward Denison deserves attention, and we summarize his analysis of the difference between northwestern Europe and the United States in 1955–62 rates of change and 1960 levels of output per worker.

Between 1955 and 1962, output per man-hour rose about 3.7 percent per annum in northwestern Europe and about 2.5 percent in the United States, after adjustments for differences in deflation procedures and in the cyclical standings of the end years. (In 1962, unemployment in the United States was much greater than in 1955, for example.) As we have already noted, there was a more rapid rate of increase in tangible capital per man-hour in Europe but a less rapid rate of increase in quality of labor force. These roughly offset one another. The larger part of the difference of about 1.2 percent therefore reflected a higher rate of increase in efficiency in Europe.

Accounting for the difference in the increase in efficiency were four groups of factors, all counted as of roughly equal importance by Denison:

1. A shift of workers out of farming and out of self-employment in the nonagricultural industries, which improved the allocation of resources in both Europe and the United States, but more there than here. This, Denison believes, was because Europe had more waste to eliminate, rather than because Europe was more successful in curtailing the waste.

2. Economies of scale resulting, first, from growth of the size of national and local markets as output rose, and second, from reductions in barriers to international trade. Economies resulted on both sides of the Atlantic, but they were greater in Europe than in the United States.

3. Reductions in hours of work. These improved the quality of work done in Europe more than that done in the United States because hours there fell from a significantly higher level and more rapidly.

4. Other factors not separately estimated, including a speed-up by northwestern Europe in its application of advanced technology and other useful knowledge to the production of goods and services—essentially a move toward catching up with the United States.

In these ways, northwestern Europe reduced the productivity gap between it and the United States by the end of the period (to judge from Denison's estimates for 1960) to about 40 percent of the United States level. The quality of European labor and the amount of Europe's tangible capital per worker were still below the corresponding United States levels. Mainly, however, the gap remained because European efficiency—though closer than in 1955—was still substantially below efficiency in the United States.

The reasons offered for the remaining difference in efficiency are, naturally, those already listed. Even after considerable progress, Europe still wasted more than the United States in agricultural employment and in non-agricultural self-employment. Though larger than in 1955, European markets were still smaller than those in the United States. The hours of work, though lower than in 1955, were still above those in the United States, and work was presumably less efficient on that account. But most important, according to Denison (accounting for something like half the gap), is the residual—the lower level of efficiency, compared with the United States, for "other reasons." Mostly, this was a "technology gap," perhaps because of a poorer quality of management in Europe, greater obstacles to modernization imposed by labor, government, or cartels, less expenditure on research and development, or still other reasons.

Much of what passes for a "technology gap" in current discussion, it should be added, is in fact a "productivity gap," to which international differences in education, tangible capital, scale of markets, efficiency in the allocation of resources among different industries, and hours of work also contribute importantly. But even what is truly a "backward" technology may reflect the absence or inadequacy of the other factors. The advanced technology of the United States is not directly available to a country that lacks the trained people, the capital, the scale of markets, or the enterprise needed to adapt the technology to local conditions and use it profitably.

CONCLUSION

W e began this *Primer on Productivity* with the statement that the facts to be weighed are among the fundamental facts of economic life. We now conclude with an even broader claim: that productivity is a fundamental factor in the quality of human existence.

True, "how a man lives with his family, his tribe or his fellow-citizens; the songs he sings; what he feels and thinks when he looks at the sunset; the prayers he raises —all these are more important than the nature of his tools, his trick of swapping things with his neighbors, the way he holds and tills his fields, his inventions and their consequences, his money . . . his savings and what he does with them." But Sir John Clapham, the great historian whom I am quoting, went on to say that "economic activity, with its tools, fields, trade, inventions and investment" has "in course of ages, provided, first for a privileged few and then for more, chances to practice high arts, organize great states, design splendid temples, or think at leisure about the meaning of the world."

How good the lives of men are depends—surely only in part, but surely also in some significant part—on the productivity of their labor.

A recognition of this basic fact, and of how far apart countries are in levels and rates of growth of productivity, has spread widely in recent decades. The gap has been made plainly visible, even exaggerated, by the Hollywood movie and then by the crowd of well-heeled tourists stepping off jet airplanes in places that hardly ever saw a foreigner before World War II. The knowledge is impelling action to reduce the differences.

Our explanation of the international productivity gap in Chapter XIV has, of course, implications for the course action should take. What will make labor more productive is, we have seen, more resources per worker. This means more of various forms of tangible capital, more capital invested in education, and more of the means to better health, all in an appropriately balanced combination. In addition—what is at least as important as more resources—is greater efficiency in the use of resources. This can come from better technology applied more widely and more promptly, from the greater specialization permitted by larger markets, and from the avoidance of the waste that results from subsidizing industries that cannot otherwise yield normal returns to the labor and capital employed by them or the waste that results from discrimination on account of race, creed, sex, or nationality, to mention just two of the many sources of waste.

How to get more resources and to make better use of resources involves strategies and details of policy that must be adapted to the peculiarities of each country's situation. But the general principles underlying sound policy are much the same everywhere. Our discussion of these principles in Chapter XII, although focused on the situation in the United States, is applicable also to the situation in other countries.

Two of the principles will bear repetition. First, policies to raise productivity should proceed on a wide front rather than concentrate on the fad currently supposed to lead to the promised land. The aim, for example, should be to expand intangible as well as tangible capital, to raise efficiency in the use of capital as well as to increase the volume of capital, to improve productivity in agriculture as well as in manufacturing.

Second, every governmental policy, whatever its primary objective, should be designed, to the extent possible, to encourage private individuals and groups, as well as governmental authorities, to conserve, expand, and use more efficiently the social resources they have in their charge. In developing countries as well as in developed countries, and in centrally planned economies as well as in free-market economies, how rapidly productivity is pushed up depends in no small degree on the incentives offered private individuals and groups to join in the effort.

The difficulties of choosing and pursuing effective policies to raise productivity are great in any country, as our discussion of the problem in the United States has already indicated. But the difficulties are especially great in the developing countries, which are under such fierce compulsion to narrow, and narrow quickly, the gap that separates them from the developed countries.

The difficulties are great because the developing countries suffer from severe handicaps in their efforts to speed up their economic growth.

Cultural factors, for example, favor family loyalty, which to a Westerner may seem to be carried too often to the point of nepotism. And cultural factors seldom favor positive attitudes toward population control, despite the urgent problem posed for many of the developing countries by extraordinary reductions in death rates and resulting surges in population—a problem far more urgent than it was in western Europe in the eighteenth and nineteenth centuries, when the population was smaller and death rates were declining more gradually. Yet it is difficult to change these and other attitudes, for in a primitive society they are often of high moral and survival value, and they may still be so in the developing countries in some degree.

Governments in many of the developing countries, to continue, are unstable and in all the newly independent countries they are inexperienced. This handicap is especially serious in an era when optimistic notions of the power of government and of the effectiveness of central planning are prevalent—an optimism only partly justified (even in developed countries) by advances in economic knowledge and in governmental organization—and governmental authorities are charged with the primary responsibility for economic growth. As a result, economic policy is often ineffective, if not worse.

In many of the newly independent countries, further, and also in some of the older developing countries, different racial, tribal, religious, regional, and other groups have yet to learn how to live together in decent harmony. When sharply divided, as is often the case, they cannot reach, or quickly reach, a stable compromise on the nature and degree of land reform, which has caused trouble in many parts of the globe; on the choice of national language, which has led to riots in India and elsewhere; on the distribution of development funds, as in Pakistan; and on the many other issues that can lead to discord or even civil war, as in Nigeria.

It is natural, also, that the new countries should place a high value on independence from "foreign influence." This often leads to policies that keep out—or even throw out—foreign "know-how," enterprise, and capital, as well as foreign "control." And other national objectives, such as high standards of social security—which even richer countries cannot always afford—though worthy in themselves, compete with the objective of rapid economic growth.

Finally, there are climatic and other factors, of which plain bad luck is not the least, that must be included even in a truncated list of handicaps. These limit the quantity and quality of available or even potential natural resources.

These handicaps are not the exclusive burden of the developing nations. In this as in other regards, the developing nations differ from the developed nations more in degree than in kind. This is apparent even in the case of cultural factors. One reason that has been offered for the technology gap between western Europe and the United States, for example, is the fact that in Europe scientists do not stoop to do the work of mere technicians, whereas in the United States scientists will seldom hesitate to make measurements themselves when it takes little extra time and trouble. Differences in social attitudes and other factors thus help to explain productivity differences among developed, as well as between developed and developing, countries. But the differences, both in productivity and in the factors that contribute to the productivity gap, are far greater between the developed and the developing countries than among those already developed.

In the fullness of time some of these handicaps may become lighter. Thus, the economic growth that is taking place everywhere and the urbanization and industrialization that inevitably accompany growth will transform values, attitudes, and institutions, as they have already done to some extent in the past. The younger generations, if not also the old, will be different. In this way the obstacles to growth will be eroded or surmounted.

But if the low-income countries are to raise their productivity rapidly enough to narrow the gap that separates them from the high-income countries, which are also raising their productivity, they will have to take a hand in speeding up the process, as more and more of them are now recognizing with respect to family planning. And they will have to learn to compromise their internal differences and slow down their drive to attain complete independence from "domination by foreign interests."

The aid of the developed countries, in the form of freer trade as well as more grants and government loans, could help. And so could better knowledge of the sources of increases in productivity, which more intensive research and education would surely bring.

But the productivity gap is wide, and the handicaps of the developing nations are severe. In the end, it may also prove necessary for the developing countries to temper their expectations somewhat and for them—and for the world powers who court them—to avoid making irresponsible promises. Such a degree of restraint is not easy in a world in which political competition within and between countries is always keen and too often unscrupulous.

BIBLIOGRAPHY

To avoid burdening the general reader, tables, charts, and other such detailed or technical material have been omitted. Many of the relevant statistics for the United States are readily available, however, in my "Basic Facts on Productivity Change," *Occasional Paper 63* (New York: National Bureau of Economic Research, 1959). Full details are given in John Kendrick's *Productivity Trends in the United States* (Princeton: Princeton University Press, 1961), published for the National Bureau of Economic Research. For the alternative U.S. estimates cited in the text, see E. F. Denison's *The Sources of Economic Growth in the United States and the Alternatives Before Us,* Supplementary Paper No. 13 (New York: Committee for Economic Development, 1962).

Productivity data for other countries are collected and analyzed in Simon Kuznets, *Modern Economic Growth* (New Haven: Yale University Press, 1966); E. F. Denison, *Why Growth Rates Differ* (Washington, D.C.: Brookings Institution, 1967); and Angus Maddison, *Economic Growth in the West* (New York: Twentieth Century Fund, 1964).

The following references will assist those readers who wish to pursue more extended discussions of particular aspects of the subject. I also include the titles of reports mentioned in the text.

A brief discussion of the relation between productivity concepts and "production functions" (relevant to the subject of Chapter I), together with a bibliography, appears in my article on "Productivity" in the *International Encyclopedia of the Social Sciences* (New York: Macmillan and Free Press, 1968). An interesting contrast of views on productivity of economists from the Soviet Union and other Communist countries with those of Western economists appears in *Labor Productivity*, ed. by J. T. Dunlop and V. P. Diatchenko (New York: McGraw-Hill, 1964). For readers prepared to cope with technical material, a discussion of concepts and measurement is given in Conference on Research in Income and Wealth, *Output, Input, and Productivity Measurement*, Studies in Income and Wealth, Vol. 25 (Princeton: Princeton University Press, 1961), published for the National Bureau of Economic Research; and, together with an up-to-date bibliography, in D. W. Jorgenson and Z. Griliches, "The Explanation of Productivity Change," *Review of Economic Studies* (1967).

The effort of the Bureau of Labor Statistics to determine the degree of acceleration in the trend of output per man-hour (described in Chapter II) is reported in BLS *Bulletin 1249* (December 1959).

Patterns of change in productivity in different industries (the topic of Chapter III) are discussed in more detail in G. J. Stigler, *Trends in Output and Employment* (New York: National Bureau of Economic Research, 1947); and in my *Employment in Manufacturing; 1899–1939: An Analysis of Its Relation to the Volume of Production* (NBER, 1942). On productivity in the service industries, see V. R. Fuchs, *The Service Economy* (NBER, 1968). Productivity in government is discussed in Chapter 5 of my *Trend of Government Activity since 1900* (NBER, 1952). The steel story (mentioned in Chapter III) is told from the industry viewpoint in Jules Backman, "Steel Prices, the Steel Industry, and the National Economy" (privately printed, 1965); and the government's position is presented in the *Report to the President on Steel Prices* by the Council of Economic Advisers (multilithed, April, 1965).

Recent research on investment in education (discussed in Chapter IV) is summarized in T. W. Schultz's *The Economic Value of Education* (New York: Columbia University Press, 1963). An important part of this research appears in G. S. Becker's *Human Capital* (NBER, 1964).

The most comprehensive discussion of tangible capital (the subject of Chapter V) will be found in Simon Kuznets, *Capital in the American Economy* (Princeton: Princeton University Press, 1961), published for the NBER. The basic statistics are in R. W. Goldsmith, *The National Wealth of the United States in the Postwar Period* (Princeton: Princeton University Press, 1962), published for the NBER; and the estimate for the most recent period, in J. W. Kendrick, "The Wealth of the Nations," *The Morgan Guaranty Survey* (August, 1966).

On technological changes (one of the topics of Chapter VI), see my "Measurement of Technological Change," *Seminar on Manpower Policy and Program,* Manpower Administration (Washington, D.C.: U.S. Department of Labor, 1965). Developments in petroleum refining are described in J. L. Enos, "Invention and Innovation in the Petroleum Industry," which is included, along with other interesting and relevant papers, in *The Rate and Direction of Inventive Activity: Economic and Social Factors* (Princeton: Princeton University Press, 1962), a conference volume published for the NBER, 1962. The papers given at the 1957 conference of the International Economic Association (also mentioned in Chapter VI) are published in *The Economic Consequences of the Size of Nations,* ed. by Austin Robinson (New York: Macmillan, 1960). The Frankfurter-Goldmark brief, *The Case for the Shorter Work Day,* Supreme Court of the United States, October Term, 1915, *Bunting* v. *The State of Oregon,* Brief for Defendant in Error, was reprinted by the National Consumers' League, Washington, D.C.

For more on productivity and business cycles (Chapter VII), see Thor Hultgren, *Cost, Prices and Profits: Their Cyclical Relations* (NBER, 1965), to which G. H. Moore provides an introduction for the general reader. An example of recent econometric work (rather too technical for the general reader) is Edwin Kuh, "Cyclical and Secular Labor Productivity in U.S. Manufacturing," *The Review of Economics and Statistics* (February, 1965).

The basic theory of wages (relevant to Chapter VIII) is in Paul Douglas, *The Theory of Wages,* reprint of 1934 edition (New York: Kelley, 1957). For the effects of trade unions on the general wage level and on the wage structure, see Albert Rees, *The Economics of Trade Unions* (Chicago: University of Chicago Press, 1962).

The relation between productivity and prices in individual industries (Chapter IX) is a major topic in all economics textbooks. Recent econometric work is illustrated by F. Q. Raines, "Price and Productivity Trends in Manufacturing Industries," *The Review of Economics and Statistics* (August, 1967).

For the report of the National Commission on Technology, Automation, and Economic Progress (noted in Chapter X), see *Technology and the American Economy,* Vol. 1 (February, 1966). See also George Terborgh, *The Automation Hysteria* (Washington, D.C.: Machinery and Allied Products Institute, 1965).

On productivity guideposts (Chapter XI), see Economic Report of the President, 1962 and later (Washington, D.C.: 1962); John Sheahan, *The Wage-Price Guideposts* (Washington, D.C.: Brookings Institution, 1967); *Guidelines: Informal Controls and the Market Place,* ed. by G. P. Shultz, and R. Z. Aliber (Chicago: University of Chicago Press, 1966); and A. F. Burns, "Wages and Prices by Formula?," Harvard Business Review (1965). For European "incomes policies" see Andrew Shonfield, *Modern Capitalism* (New York: Oxford University Press, 1965). The bearing of change in labor quality on the wage guidepost is pointed out in my paper, "Which Productivity?," *Monthly Labor Review* (June, 1962).

For an excellent discussion of policy to raise productivity (the subject of Chapter XII), see A. F. Burns' lecture on "Planning for Economic Growth in the United States," published in pamphlet form by DePauw University, April, 1962. The report of the Advisory Commission on Intergovernmental Relations (mentioned in Chapter XII) is *Building Codes: A Program for Intergovernmental Reform* (Washington, D.C.: January, 1966).

The best general discussion of the international productivity gap (and an important source for Chapter XIV), is Denison's *Why Growth Rates Differ,* already cited. Denison confines himself to a comparison of the United States and western Europe. For U.S.A.–U.S.S.R. comparisons, see Abram Bergson, *The Economics of Soviet Planning* (New Haven: Yale University Press, 1964), and J. S. Berliner, "The Static Efficiency of the Soviet Economy," *American Economic Review* (May, 1964).

The paragraph quoted in the Conclusion is from Sir John Clapham's *A Concise Economic History of Britain* (New York: Cambridge University Press, 1949).

ACKNOWLEDGMENTS

I am greatly indebted to three institutions, none of which is responsible for my interpretation of the facts or the opinions expressed in this book, but without which I could not have written it: New York University, where the lectures on which this book is based were first presented; the National Bureau of Economic Research, whose staff did a great deal of the research underlying the lectures; and the Alfred P. Sloan Foundation, which financed my visits to Productivity Centers abroad and encouraged my efforts at a popular account of the researches on productivity that the foundation had been patiently supporting at the National Bureau. Because institutions work through people, I direct my thanks to Dean Joseph H. Taggart of the Graduate School of Business Administration of NYU and to the students who listened to me at GBA; Dr. Arthur F. Burns and other colleagues at the National Bureau; and Dr. Arnold J. Zurcher, Vice-President of the Sloan Foundation.

I owe a debt also to the Maurice and Laura Falk Foundation and its director, J. Steele Gow, for support of my initial studies of productivity at the National Bureau; to Haig Babian, editor of *Challenge Magazine,* for permission to use here several sections first edited and published by him in *Challenge* in a preliminary form; and to Peter Bernstein, who read and made constructive comments on the manuscript as a whole.

I have barely begun to state my obligations, either here or (by implication) in the bibliography. While the full list of persons to whom I am indebted is too long for inclusion here, I must at least record my gratitude to them.

INDEX

About the Author

In introducing Solomon Fabricant's contribution to a symposium on productivity and wages published in Harvard University's Review of Economics and Statistics, the Editor called him an "outstanding economist and statistician who has done brilliant work in this field." Dr. Fabricant's first major study of productivity, Employment in Manufacturing, 1899–1939: An Analysis of Its Relation to the Volume of Production, was completed just before World War II. This volume was followed by over a score of other publications on productivity, ranging from Productivity of Labor in Peace and War (1942) to the authoritative article, "Productivity," in the new International Encyclopedia of the Social Sciences (1968).

Dr. Fabricant is Professor of Economics at New York University. He is also a member of the Senior Research Staff of the National Bureau of Economic Research, for which he served as Director of Research for twelve years. During World War II he was with the War Production Board in Washington and UNRWA in London. He was Chairman of the first Productivity Conference sponsored by the Bureau of Labor Statistics and the Bureau of the Budget and has lectured at universities in Brazil, Japan, India, and other countries. He has been a Vice President of the American Economic Association, a member of the Board of Editors of the American Statistical Association, and Chairman of the Research Advisory Board of the Committee for Economic Development.

A Note on the Type

The text of this book was set on the Linotype in Baskerville. Linotype Baskerville is a facsimile cutting from type cast from the original matrices of a face designed by John Baskerville. The original face was the forerunner of the "modern" group of type faces.

John Baskerville (1706–75), of Birmingham, England, a writing-master, with a special renown for cutting inscriptions in stone, began experimenting about 1750 with punch-cutting and making typographical material. It was not until 1757 that he published his first work. His types, at first criticized, in time were recognized as both distinct and elegant, and his types as well as his printing were greatly admired.

Composed, printed, and bound by The Colonial Press, Inc., Clinton, Mass.